Last Chance Ranch

Last Chance Ranch Book 1

Liz Isaacson

ISBN-13: 978-1638761457

Chapter One

Scarlett Adams wiped her dirty hands down the front of her jeans, wondering what her life had become. She'd only been at Last Chance Ranch for two weeks, but it felt worlds different than the life she'd left in Los Angeles, only thirty miles away.

That couldn't be right. Thirty miles?

She sighed and scraped her sweaty flyaways off her forehead. Surely this place was at least three universes from the life she'd known on Earth.

This was your choice, she told herself as she surveyed the room holding more stuff than she'd ever owned in her life. Yes, her mother had called her and said her grandfather needed help. And Scarlett had seized the opportunity to leave the city, something she'd been wanting to do since her divorce had become final.

No, she wasn't wearing skirts and silks and heels

anymore. She'd thought those things made her happy, but she knew now that they didn't. Of course, neither did sleeping as late as she wanted, wearing jeans all the time, and cleaning out years of her grandfather's hoard.

So maybe she hadn't thought through this life choice as much as she should have. But how was she to know Gramps hadn't thrown anything away since Grams had died? It wasn't like Scarlett came out to the ranch all that often, despite the short distance from her previous apartment to this sprawling piece of land in the Glendora foothills, right at the base of the Angeles National Forest.

She was still in California—it only felt like she'd blasted off to the moon and was trying to organize it.

She picked up a jar with an unknown substance in it, hoping it was well-sealed and would stay that way. Probably something Grams had canned decades ago. Maybe grape juice. Scarlett wasn't entirely sure, and she wasn't going to find out. She'd rented an industrial-sized dumpster that she filled faster than the sanitation department would come pick it up. She'd made great progress on the ranch, getting the homestead cleaned out, as well as the three spare cabins that sat just behind the main house.

There were thirteen other cabins that sat near the entrance of the ranch, along with that robot mailbox she'd loved as a little girl. She smiled thinking about the contraption her great-grandfather had welded together and which her older brother had dubbed Prime, because he'd been learning about prime numbers in school at the time and there was only one robot mailbox like the one guarding Last Chance Ranch.

Those cabins had been empty for a while, and Scarlett hadn't done much to them to make sure they were habitable. If she wanted to save Last Chance Ranch, she'd need to fill them with men and women willing to work. She'd need to find a way to pay those people. And she'd need to figure out how to get Gramps to let go of some of the stuff he thought he couldn't live without.

Scarlett knew what he was doing wasn't considered living. And she knew that what he couldn't live without he couldn't get back. Grams.

Another sigh left her mouth, and she gently set the jar of whatever-it-was in the wheelbarrow she was using to haul trash from what used to be a sun room to the dumpster. Oh, yes, this would be a sun room again, and she'd sit here with Gramps while he drank black coffee and she sipped chamomile tea. Oh, yes....

She dug back into the work, ignoring the sun as it continued to beat down on her. Item by item piled into the wheelbarrow until she tried to lift it and could barely do so. She hefted it into position and started for the dumpster, which was concealed on the east side of the homestead. That way, when the director for Forever Friends, the animal organization Scarlett had contacted to come see the facilities at the ranch, arrived, she wouldn't see all the trash.

In fact, Scarlett was hoping to get all the trash off the

premises before Jewel Nightingale showed up. Considering that the woman hadn't even responded to one of Scarlett's emails or phone calls kept her resting easy at night.

Oh, and all this physical labor. That certainly had her sleeping like a baby in a way her marketing executive job never had.

She passed a half a dozen cars and trucks on her trek from Gramps's place to the garbage container, and she had no idea what to do about those. Gramps claimed none of them ran, and Scarlett certainly didn't have the skill set to fix them. She could probably sell them and get some much-needed cash for the ranch if she could get any of the engines to turn over.

"At least Gramps has all the keys," she muttered as she approached the trash bin. She couldn't lift the wheelbarrow up and over the lip of the dumpster, so she'd been throwing items in one at a time, or shoveling them in with a strong, plastic snow shovel she'd found in one of the barns.

How Gramps had ever bought a snow shovel in California, Scarlett wasn't sure. But it worked great to get trash up and into the container.

In the distance, dogs barked from their runs in the area of the ranch Scarlett had affectionately called the Canine Club. Gramps loved the dogs too, and he spent most of his time with them on the north side of the ranch. When she'd asked him how many dogs lived on the ranch, he'd said, "Maybe twenty."

"Maybe?" Scarlett hadn't meant to screech the word. "You don't know how many dogs live here?"

"There's at least twenty," he'd said again. And so, when Scarlett's muscles screamed at her to stop using them so strenuously, she'd go out to the different regions of the ranch—Canine Club, Feline Frenzy, Horse Heaven, Piggy Paradise, and LlamaLand—and document what lived there. What breeds, if she could figure it out. How many dogs, cats, llamas, horses.

She'd searched on the Internet and asked Gramps dozens of questions about what the animals ate and how he paid for the food. He seemed to have a schedule of volunteers coming out every day, seven days a week, to walk dogs and play with cats.

Oh, and the ranch had come with exactly one cowboy —a man named Sawyer Smith who gave horseback riding lessons on Saturday mornings, took care of the horses and cattle, and managed the majority of the crops on the ranch.

Scarlett had hardly ever seen Sawyer in the two weeks she'd been at Last Chance Ranch, and that was just fine with her. At forty-three-years-old, she was not interested in another romance. Nope. Not happening.

She finished unloading the last of the trash from the wheelbarrow, the thought of returning to go through more garbage almost so depressing she could fall to her knees.

But she didn't. She kept her back straight and clapped her work gloves together, sending dirt and dust into the air.

The dogs were really barking up a storm.

Scarlett left the wheelbarrow behind as she stepped onto the dirt lane in front of the homestead and started down it. Another road forked to the left a ways up, and that led to Canine Club and several barns where the goats lived.

If she were being honest, goats terrified her, and she'd never been happier to have brought a friend with her to the ranch. Adele Woodruff had worked in the city with Scarlett, and she'd needed a fresh start somewhere with less smog—and less likelihood of a debt collector showing up while she was trying to answer phones. Adele lived in the cabin right next door to Gramps, and she'd been tending to the goats, claiming she had a great way to start bringing in cash for the ranch.

She wouldn't tell Scarlett what it was though, but she worked in the pastures and goat arena for hours with the animals.

Scarlett didn't see her as she passed the cat houses and entered the Canine Club. "What's going on?" she asked Annie, a white bulldog mix who seemed to be the matron of the club. "Where's Gramps?"

She opened the gate and entered the dog community, where she'd documented a whopping twenty-six dogs lived. "Maybe twenty" had been way off, and the budget to feed and care for these dogs exceeded what Gramps brought in from his social security and Grams's death benefit.

Scarlett really needed the partnership of Forever Friends, and she needed it quickly. After deciding she'd call Jewel again once she got back to where she could wash her hands, Scarlett pushed her fear away.

She had a lot of savings, and while she'd lost a lot in the divorce, it wasn't all monetary. She wouldn't allow herself to think of Billy and Bob for more than a moment. A quick whisper of thought, and then gone. It hurt too much that she didn't have her own fur babies with her on this ranch where twenty-six other dogs lived. Billy and Bob would've loved the Canine Club, and they should've been there with her.

"Gramps?" she called, the moment where she thought of her own dogs over.

He didn't answer, but a distinctly male voice said, "Hey, do you own this place?"

Scarlett spun toward the voice to find a tall, dreamy man wearing a cowboy hat and holding a leash.

"Scooby?" she asked, sure this man's name wasn't the cartoon character. "What are you doing with my dog?" Anger and iciness was the only defense she'd have against this man, she could tell.

"He was out on the road," the man said, glancing down at the big brown boxer. "Hound managed to make friends with him while I got the leash on."

Scarlett noticed the golden retriever at the man's side

—no leash required. So he had enough charm to make dogs do things according to his command. Of course he did. Scarlett felt his charisma and charm tingling way down in her toes.

"I wasn't sure if he came from up here or not. I just followed the sound of all the barking."

"He belongs here," Scarlett said, stepping forward to take the leash from him. "Scooby, you've got to stop digging under the fences." And not just because Scarlett struggled to fill in the holes.

"I'm Hudson Flannigan," the man said, reaching up with his now-free hand to lift his cowboy hat and push his hair back. He had dark sideburns and at least three days' worth of a beard to match his salt-and-pepper hair, and Scarlett's heart betrayed her by sending out a couple of extra beats.

He was her age.

So what? she asked herself in a harsh mental voice. She was used to looking for and finding details no one else did, and this man clearly hadn't bathed in a couple of days. Probably as long as it had taken to grow that sexy scruff.

She gave herself a mental shake as she found tattered cuffs on his jeans, the well-worn cowboy boots, the soft sparkle in his eyes. And the hint of grease under his fingernails.

"I noticed your mailbox on the way in," he said, that voice like melting butter.

"What of it?" she asked, trying to keep a grip on

Scooby, who probably weighed as much as she did. She almost scoffed out loud. That so wasn't true. She was no lightweight, and though she'd lost ten pounds since coming to the ranch and starting the physical labor, she was easily still a size fourteen.

"It looked like it could use a tune-up," he said. "Some of the pieces need to be welded together again."

She narrowed her eyes at him. "And I suppose you're just the man to do it." Did he wander the foothills, looking for jobs?

"I could," he said. "I'm a master welder and I'm not bad with horses either." His dog laid down, his tongue out like this was the most boring conversation on the planet.

An idea formed in Scarlett's mind. She definitely needed help with the horses. She'd been tending to them every morning and evening, but she had no idea what she was doing. "We have sixteen horses here at the ranch," she said. "I have a guy who does riding lessons on the weekend."

Hudson nodded and touched the brim of his hat as if to say, *Point taken. You don't need me.*

"I can't pay you much," Scarlett said quickly. "But I have a clean cabin you can live in. Hound too. And you can fix that mailbox, work with Sawyer in Horse Heaven, and...." She cocked her head, sure she was right about him. "How handy are you with cars?"

Chapter Two

I f Hudson Flannigan had been doubting why he'd turned up this obscure road when he'd heard a dog bark, he quit the moment that auburn-haired beauty asked him how handy he was with cars.

"I do all right," he said evasively. He didn't need to go showing his whole hand at once. He also couldn't help the steady prayer that started in his head and wouldn't stop.

Please, please, Lord. I need this job. Please help me get this job.

Over and over the words looped through his mind. Of course, if God cared all that much about Hudson, his marriage of ten years wouldn't have fallen apart. Or at least the Lord would've given him a clue that his wife was being unfaithful. Or maybe the fact that Hudson had lived so long in unknowing bliss had been more merciful of the Lord. The jury was still out on that one.

And Hudson had been down and out since the divorce, almost a year ago now. He hadn't stayed in one place longer than a couple of months, and the constant travel was tiring.

The woman nodded toward his hands. "Looks like you've worked on one recently."

"Just my truck," he said, wanting to hide his hands.

"Well, I'm Scarlett Adams, and I'm running this ranch with my grandfather. He's got at least six vehicles on the property that need fixing, and if you do it, I'll split the profit with you."

Hudson's eyebrows went up. "What kind of split?"

"Eighty-twenty," she said without missing a beat.

He scoffed, almost offended but enjoying this game with Scarlett too much. "You're joking, right?"

"We own the vehicles. They just don't run."

"Which makes them useless," he said. "I'll go...eighty-twenty in my favor."

She gaped at him, those beautiful eyes like pools of pond water he could dive into and swim around in. When she started laughing, Hudson smiled.

"You're a funny guy," she said, still giggling and still holding onto that boxer like she was trying to choke him.

Hudson stepped forward and took the leash from her. He let it slacken and hang at his side, saying, "Stay, Scooby." The dog stayed. "I'll just help you get him back inside then," he said. "I didn't own and operate my own mechanic shop for twenty years to fix someone else's cars and not get paid for it."

He moved past her, hoping she'd counteroffer. A place to live out on this beautiful land sounded mighty appealing.

Please, he thought again, wishing the last time he'd been to church wasn't a month ago. But surely God understood why Hudson hadn't gone. It was hard when people asked where he lived and he couldn't give them an address.

He tried opening the door to the building she'd been standing in front of, but it was locked. Just like last time he'd tried. Maybe this gorgeous woman had distracted him too much.

"It takes a key card," she said, squeezing in beside him and swiping a card in front of the reader. The door clicked, and she gestured for him to go in.

He did, his head swimming with the strawberry scent of her hair. She was dirty too, and somehow that added to her allure. "Where do you want him?"

"Over here." She stepped over to one of the empty pens in the circular room. With ease, she pulled the bolt up and the gate swung in.

Hudson unclipped Hound's leash from around the other dog's neck and said, "Go on." Scooby moved into the pen, and Scarlett locked him inside before facing Hudson again.

"Fifty-fifty," she said.

"I want to see the cars," he said.

Her eyes blazed with fire that wasn't entirely angry, but that he knew would burn him just the same. And he didn't mind. In fact, he thought he might like to be torched by this woman.

No, you don't want that, he told himself. He'd been operating on half a heart since Jan's betrayal. He hadn't been able to go home, as his mom loved Jan as much as him. In fact, since the divorce, she'd hosted a birthday party for his ex-wife and they still played Bunko together monthly.

Hudson had always been a disappointment to his horse-training father, who didn't understand how any son of his could be content with being a mechanic. So Hudson had wandered from San Diego to Sacramento, looking for odd jobs, anything that would fill the tank in his truck and get him something to eat.

Another day. Another dollar. Another job.

"Fine," Scarlett clipped out. "Come with me."

"C'mon, Hound," he said as he followed the curvy woman back outside. The view was certainly better than any he'd had in a while, and he found another smile forming on his face.

His pulse seemed to start with the pleadings, every beat pushing out a *please-please. Help-me. Please-Lord.*

Scarlett marched down the road, Hudson matching

her stride for stride. "There's a couple of trucks," she said. "Four cars, and that's all in the main yard. There's tractors and stuff in the equipment shed, though Sawyer says those run okay."

"And do they?" he asked.

"I don't really know," she said. "I think everything around here needs a lot of attention and a good cleaning, the vehicles included." She shot him a look out of the corner of her eye that he wasn't sure if it was a glare or just a glance. "I've only been here for two weeks, and Gramps...well, Gramps is eighty-one-years-old, and a hoarder."

Compassion ran through Hudson. She was stepping into a situation she couldn't control. And making the best of it. Hudson had some experience with that, and he knew what kind of grit and determined spirit a person had to possess to do it.

"There they are," she said, going around the corner of the house and stopping.

He paused too and took in the row of vehicles in front of him. The trucks were old—older than him, and maybe as old as her grandpa. If he could get those running, they'd fetch a lot of money.

The cars seemed to be old sedans, nothing important or all that note-worthy. But if they ran, and the upholstery was in good shape, he could get a few thousand for them. People bought cars like that for their teenagers all the time.

The numbers added up in his head, and he'd take fifty percent if she'd give it to him. He said, "Those cars aren't worth anything. The trucks, maybe. Seventy-thirty."

"Sixty-forty."

"For me?"

"For you."

Hudson peered at the row of vehicles like he was really thinking about it. Several long moments passed, and then he said, "Deal."

She turned toward him, that long dark red hair swinging in its ponytail. "Deal." She extended her hand and he took it, ignoring the fizz of attraction now simmering in his bloodstream.

They shook hands, and she said, "I'll get the paperwork drawn up. Do you want to see the cabin?"

AN HOUR LATER, Hudson filled Hound's bowl with fresh, cold water from the hose on the side of his new cabin. He left the dog to drink as he went up the back steps and into the cabin Scarlett had let him choose for himself.

There were thirteen almost identical cabins here at Last Chance Ranch, and he'd chosen the one in the corner of the U-shaped arrangement. It had a bigger yard for Hound, and a row of huge oak trees along the grass that would shade his place from the setting Western sun.

"Thank you," he whispered to the empty room, the kitchen on his right, dining room on his left, and living room in front of him. The cabin was a box, with a hallway that led to a bedroom and a bathroom on the other side of the kitchen. So not somewhere he'd live and raise a family, but for him and Hound, it was perfect.

Absolutely perfect.

It had running water, which meant he could shower every day. A washing machine and dryer took up space in the bathroom, which meant he could wash his clothes whenever he wanted. There was a single couch in the living room, a table with two chairs in the dining room, and a bed, so he didn't have to live in the back of his truck with the camper shell anymore.

His was full-size, and he could stand up almost all the way right in the doorway. If he wasn't so tall, he'd be fine. His bed sat at the back of the truck bed, and he passed a kitchen with a microwave, sink, and two-burner stove on his left to get to the bed. He had plenty of storage for his stuff, and a bench he could sit on to put on his boots. But no toilet. The shower had a twenty-gallon tank that stayed hot when he decided to use it. He also had a built-in heater and air conditioner in the shell. Not that he needed the temperature regulators in May in California. He had used the heater a few times on rainy days in the winter, especially farther north.

He'd been eating a lot of microwaveable meals and

canned foods, already prepared things like granola bars and bags of chips, and as he gazed at the full-sized stove and oven in the kitchen of this cabin, he thought he'd died and gone to heaven.

He could cook. He could do laundry. He could bathe. Hudson had never been happier, and he bent to retrieve his backpack so he could get out his charger, plug in his phone, and get it powered up while he showered. Then he'd call his brother Brent and tell him all about the stray dog that had provided him the opportunity to be proud of himself again.

After all, in the course of the last couple of hours, he'd gotten a job. A place to live that wasn't on wheels. And a pretty redhead who kept popping up in his mind's eye, despite her frosty reception of him.

He frowned into the warm spray of the shower—his best bath in months, by the way. He wasn't looking for another girlfriend. His heart and life had been through the shredder lately, and he just needed something stable to figure out how to be the new Hudson now that he wasn't part of a couple.

The past year had been one of great learning for him, but it was mostly how to be by himself. He wasn't sure who he was without Jan, or how to be that person in a permanent place. It was easier to be a good person and be kind when he was just passing through.

Now, though, he'd have to figure out how to be kind

and good and Christ-like when he saw the same people day after day.

Refreshed from his shower, he went out to his truck and got his welding tools together, determined to get his first job on this ranch complete. When he opened the front door, he found Scarlett coming up the steps with an older gentleman on her arm.

With her eyes down, she didn't see him immediately, so he said, "Hey, let me help." He moved to help her grandfather up the steps, and the old man looked up with pale blue, watery eyes.

"Gramps wanted to meet you," Scarlett said. "He said Scooby is his favorite dog, and he's just so grateful you found him and brought him back." Her voice carried a measure of sarcasm and she rolled her eyes halfway when Hudson looked at her.

"Oh, it was no problem," Hudson said, his kindest voice employed. He smiled at Scarlett and then her grandpa. "I'm just glad I found where he belonged." He looped his hand through the old man's arm too and steadied him as he moved up the steps.

"Gramps, this is Hudson Flannigan. He's going to fix up all the vehicles on the ranch." She beamed at her grandfather and then Hudson, the brightness of her smile fading a bit when their eyes locked.

But for Hudson, his whole soul lit up like a solar flare, and he had a hard time tearing his eyes from hers.

"Good, good," her grandfather said. "That lawn

mower stopped working a few weeks ago, too. Maybe he could look at that."

"I could," Hudson said as a feeling that he'd just signed on for a heck of a lot more than he'd thought. This ranch needed a lot of work—it was called Last Chance Ranch, after all. And Hudson definitely felt like he was on his last chance.

Chapter Three

W atching Hudson interact with Gramps was entirely unfair. He talked with him like they'd known each other for years, not just a few minutes. And they used words she didn't understand the meaning of, like "carburetor" and "late-model Ford."

Why couldn't they just speak English? Why did Hudson have to be so handsome in that cowboy hat? Why did his cologne have to fire up every dormant female cell in her body?

Scarlett had argued with Gramps for fifteen minutes before giving in and driving him over to what she'd dubbed the Community. Well, Hudson was the only member so far, but Sawyer was planning to move into one of the cabins instead of commuting from nearby Pasadena. And Adele lived here now, though not over in these cabins.

She figured if she gave Gramps what he wanted in regard to meeting Hudson, next time she wanted to throw away something he claimed he needed, she could use this to get rid of it. She didn't want to hurt her grandfather, but the pile of items they could sell was growing and growing, and they needed the money.

Hudson served ice water and offered her and Gramps granola bars. Scarlett declined, and not just because oats and honey went straight to her hips. She didn't want to eat in front of Hudson yet, her insecurities about her plus-sized body rearing their ugly heads.

Of course he's not interested in you, her mind whispered to her as they made small talk. Gramps fell asleep within minutes, leaving Hudson talking to himself and Scarlett trying to figure out what emotion she'd seen in his eyes as they'd come up the steps.

"So where are you from?" he asked, lifting his water glass to his lips.

"LA," she said. "Well, really a bit south of there. Newport Beach. My parents live there still. I worked as a marketing executive at a firm in LA for a long time before coming here." She pressed her lips together, thinking the granola bar would've stopped her from spewing so much about herself in a single breath. "You?" she squeaked out, realizing she knew absolutely nothing about this man. He could be an axe murderer for all she knew, and she'd just hired him and given him a place to live.

"My shop was in Santa Monica," he said.

"Oh, right on the coast."

"Yes." He seemed to be experiencing the smell and splash of the ocean as he stared at something past her. Then he shook himself and said, "It did well for a lot of years."

"So why don't you have it anymore?" Scarlett shot a glance at her still-snoozing grandpa. She really didn't have time to sit on this lumpy couch and make small talk. But she couldn't get herself to leave.

"I sold it after the divorce," he said, taking another long drink of water.

"Oh," she said. "I'm sorry to hear that." She watched him, and he looked sorry too for about a second.

"Yes, well, I didn't want to be cheated on again." Pain definitely crossed his face this time, and Scarlett wondered how long it had been since the divorce. But she wasn't going to ask.

"I'm divorced too," she blurted, wishing she could suck the words back in. "It's been going on for about three years now, and was just finalized about four months ago." She heard the discomfort in her own voice, but she couldn't erase it. Didn't even know how.

"I'm sorry," he said. "It sounds like it didn't go well."

"We fought over our dogs," she said. "That's why it took so long." She crossed her arms over her chest, trying to keep the perfect storm of emotions inside.

"No fighting in mine," he said. "Jan had already moved in with her other boyfriend by the time I filed."

Surprise filled Scarlett, and she didn't know what to say. "Some people suck," she said, which caused Hudson to chuckle.

"Yes," he said, smiling. "Some people do." He leaned forward in the chair he'd brought in from the dining room. "You're not one of them, are you, Scarlett?"

The way he said her name made her want to do nothing but sit on this couch and talk with him. Which meant she had to get up and leave. Now.

"I try not to be," she said, thinking of the red brick church Gramps had dragged her to the past couple of Sundays. Why couldn't she get herself to stand up and go?

"Me too," Hudson said. "I was going to go get started on that mailbox, but I'm pretty tired." He hooked his thumb at Gramps. "So maybe I'll just stay here and nap with him. Bring him back when he wakes up?"

He was offering her a way out, and part of Scarlett didn't want to take it. Another part did, so she scooted to the edge of the couch and stood up. "That would be great. He lives in the eastern-most cabin behind the homestead."

"Are you in the homestead?" Hudson asked, following her to the front door.

"That's right," she said.

"And it's just me, you, Gramps, and Sawyer."

"And my friend Adele," Scarlett said. "She lives next door to Gramps. I'm going to be hiring more people. We're doing okay with what we have, but we need help." She looked at him, thinking maybe he knew people who needed a job.

"So five humans. Sixteen horses. A bunch of dogs. I saw goats too, and I definitely smelled pigs," he said.

"And don't forget the cats and the llamas," Scarlett said. "There are over one hundred animals here at Last Chance Ranch. I'm trying to get Forever Friends to name us a rescue ranch so we can get some funding."

Something like disbelief crossed his rugged face, which was now clean-shaven. Scarlett almost reached up and slid her fingers down his smooth skin, stopping herself at the last moment. Definitely time to go.

With the heat of the sun on her back, she stepped out of his house. "How about I get your number so I can come get Gramps?"

"Oh, I'll just bring him back when he wakes up." Hudson smiled like he was trying to save her the trouble. Maybe he didn't want to give her his number. His way of saying, *No thanks, but nice try.*

"He won't wake up until morning," Scarlett said, her voice a bit harder now. "So I'll just come down in an hour and get him." She turned and shaded her eyes against the setting sun. "It'll still be light then."

Scarlett went down the steps and tossed a, "Thanks Hudson," over her shoulder as she practically sprinted away from his house. Well, her house. The cabin on the ranch, which she now owned.

The weight of the world seemed to press into her

shoulders as she walked down the road and turned to go down another one. Five cabins lined this street, with a grassy area across from them. Even if she could get enough cowboys to fill these cabins, she wasn't sure she'd ever get caught up with the work that needed to be done here.

She banished the defeating thoughts and told herself to focus on the positive. Focus on what she could control, not what she couldn't. Gramps took care of the dogs. Adele took care of the goats and the cats. Sawyer took care of the horses and cattle, leaving Scarlett to the llamas and pigs—which felt about right, actually.

So Hudson would focus on the vehicles, and as the summer continued day by day, bit by bit, Scarlett would get Last Chance Ranch up and running, if it was the last thing she did.

Because she needed just one more chance. *Please, Lord,* she prayed as she turned toward the homestead. "Everyone here just needs one last chance...."

From dogs, to llamas, to humans, this ranch provided a small piece of safety and security when they couldn't find it anywhere else. At least Scarlett wanted it to, and she made a mental to-do list as she walked.

First up? Email Jewel Nightingale at Forever Friends again.

"I DON'T KNOW, ADELE," Scarlett said the next morning, stirring another spoonful of sugar into her coffee. In the city, she'd rarely drank the stuff, but since coming to the ranch, she found she needed more than tea to make it through the day.

But when that sun room was finished, she was definitely going to sit there and bask in the golden warmth of the day, tea cup in her hand. That day was not today, and she had eleven potbellied pigs waiting for their breakfast.

"But you emailed her again, right?" Adele sat at the bar, her own coffee cup in front of her, both hands wrapped around it like it was cold that day. Which it wasn't. Her straight, chin-length hair wouldn't go into a ponytail, and not for lack of trying.

"Yes." Scarlett sighed. "I emailed her again, and I called and left a message last night. It was after five, though." She shrugged and looked at her friend. "I hired a guy to fix the cars in the yard."

"Great," she said without missing a beat. "Maybe he can look at my car too. It's making that pinging sound again."

"What are you planning on with the goats?" Scarlett asked, and Adele opened her mouth to answer. All at once, she snapped her lips closed again.

"You almost got me."

"I sure did." Scarlett smiled and sipped her coffee. "And you go down to town entirely too much. What are you buying down there?"

"Groceries," Adele said evasively.

"Groceries?" Scarlett didn't take her eyes from her best friend. "Honey, I know we like to eat, but nobody eats that much."

Adele laughed and tucked her hair behind her ear, where it would just pop back out in a few seconds. "Hey, I've lost twelve pounds since coming to the middle of nowhere."

It was Scarlett's turn to laugh, and she did, loudly and for several seconds. "Adele, this isn't the middle of nowhere. It's five minutes down the road to a gas station."

"A dirt road," Adele said. "And you look like you've lost some weight too."

"Ten pounds," Scarlett said. "I haven't dropped a jean size though."

"So this new guy...does he like curvy women?"

"I have no idea," Scarlett said. "I barely got his name. He said he owned a car shop in Santa Monica, and I was like, 'you're hired.' I need those cars off the lawn, and we need the money to feed the billions of animals here."

Adele scoffed. "So you're telling me this man isn't good looking?"

"I don't know," Scarlett said again. "And besides, I'm not looking for a date." Her memory flashed back to last night when he wouldn't give her his phone number. When she'd gone back to get Gramps, the exchange had happened quickly as Hudson had been on the phone. His brother. Whatever. Scarlett had brothers too, thank you very much.

"Are you looking for a date?" Scarlett asked, her eyebrows going up. "Want me to introduce you?"

She watched as Adele wrestled with herself, the battle lasting only a few moments before she said, "No, of course not."

"I mean, Hudson's definitely better than Jackson."

"I'm not looking for a date," Adele said. "Period."

"Good. Neither am I," Scarlett said. "That's why we came up here, isn't it?" A sliver of doubt passed through her, and Scarlett didn't like them. So Hudson was handsome. Devilishly handsome. With facial hair and without. With that dark cowboy hat and without. So he smelled good. Oh, so good. Didn't mean she wanted a taste of him.

"Hello," Adele said, making the two-syllable word into three. "I asked if you were going to put out any more help wanted ads."

"Yes," Scarlett said, giving herself a mental shake. She didn't have room for Hudson in her mind, not with the dozens of tasks she had to complete that day. And up first were those pigs and llamas, and then she had a date with the plastic snow shovel.

"Good, because I need help with the goats, and you need at least three more people to help Gramps with the dogs."

"Really?"

"Really," Adele said as she slid off the barstool. "He

loves those dogs, sure. But they need more exercise than he can give them, and even the volunteers aren't enough."

"Plus, they always seem to be in the cat houses."

"Well, they're air conditioned," Adele said. "That's where I'd be too."

"The dog enclosures are temperature regulated," Scarlett said, going down the back steps.

"Well, they're supposed to be," Adele said. "Can your mechanic look into that?" She cast Scarlett one last look before heading for the corner of the house and turning north toward the goat fields and pens.

Scarlett heaved in a deep breath and faced east, where the pigs and llamas lived. When she stepped from grass to dirt road, her phone buzzed in her back pocket. She pulled it out and checked the number, but it wasn't one she had stored in her phone.

Forever Friends, she thought, and she swiped the phone on a moment later. "Hello?"

"Scarlett?" a man asked—definitely not Jewel Nightingale.

"Yes," she said slowly. She hadn't even placed a help wanted ad yet, so who was calling her that wouldn't be in her phone? She'd wanted to erase everyone she'd worked with and been friends with. Really make a clean break from everything she'd had in her life when she'd been part of Scarlett and Vance, Vance and Scarlett.

But she hadn't. She'd taken a baby step and left the city. Another one when she'd accepted Gramps's offer to sign the ranch over to her. Another one every day she stayed here and cleaned and worked and didn't run back to Los Angeles.

"It's Hudson," he said. "And I think you better get down here."

Chapter Four

"Down where?" The panic in Scarlett's voice wasn't hard to hear. "And how did you get my number?"

"I looked up the number of the ranch online," he said, turning and pacing back toward the mailbox—if it could be called that anymore. "I was working on the mailbox, and...." He didn't want to say the whole thing had fallen apart, but the whole thing had fallen apart. Hound seemed utterly nonplussed as he lay panting in the grass, but Hudson felt the buzz of energy in his blood.

"I'll be right there," she said, and the line went dead.

Hudson let his phone drop to his side, hoping and praying this mailbox wasn't a family heirloom. But the way it had rusted and fallen apart at his first touch spoke of how long it had been standing at the entrance of this ranch.

Worry gnawed at his stomach in the few minutes it

took for Scarlett to arrive. She showed up on a four-wheeler, dirt and rocks skidding under the tires as she braked to a sloppy stop. Hound got up as if she'd come to see him, but she didn't even glance at him. "What—?"

But she didn't finish, because she caught sight of the dismembered robot. "Prime." She took a couple of steps but stopped. "What happened?"

"I literally touched his leg," Hudson said. "I swear. Just to see how loose it was. Everything fell apart."

Scarlett looked at him, her eyes blazing. "Well, fix him."

"I'm not sure—okay," he said. "I'll fix him, but he might...not be exactly the same. Some of this metal is rusted clean through."

"There's plenty of metal around the ranch," Scarlett said. "My great-grandfather built that mailbox, and...." She wiped her hand through her hair, smoothing back the wispy pieces that were too short to go into the bun on top of her head. "Get it close to what it looked like before."

Hudson nodded. "I'll do that."

Scarlett stared at him for another moment, and then she stomped over to the ATV, swung her leg over, and practically ran over the robot as she swung wildly around.

Hudson watched her go, his emotion choked up in the back of his throat. *Get it close.* He could certainly try, and he was glad he'd taken a quick picture with his phone the day before when he'd found the boxer and walked up the road to the ranch.

He pulled out his phone and swiped to find the picture. Really, all he needed was a couple of legs, a gallon of black paint, and a new bottom for the mailbox. That robot couldn't even hold mail now, and Hudson could see that if he had white and red paint too, he could really bring him back to life.

Prime.

He wondered if Scarlett had named the robot or if someone else had. He wondered a lot of things about her, including if she'd go out with him if he'd ask. But her divorce was only four months old, and Hudson wasn't sure he quite knew what he wanted himself.

He pulled out his phone and sent a text to the number he'd called. *Where might I find some metal?*

He had her number now, and she had his, and Hudson smiled as he put her name into his phone. Her response bore her name when it came in, and that made him grin too. *There's a huge pile by the hay barn.*

Hudson didn't ask where the hay barn was. He knew what a barn looked like, and he could enjoy the morning sunshine as he walked. "Come on, Hound," he said to his dog, and they set off down the road.

After about thirty minutes of wandering around the ranch and all the buildings he could see, he was forced to text Scarlett again. *Where might the hay barn be?*

It's out in the middle of LlamaLand, Horse Heaven, and Piggy Paradise. Southeast of the homestead.

"Llama Land?" He looked down at Hound, but the

golden retriever didn't point him in the right direction. Hudson hadn't gone past the horse...what was it? He checked his phone again. "Horse Heaven."

He hadn't gone that way, because it just looked like farmland, pastures, and the wilds for as far as he could see. But he walked south down the road past the homestead now, Hound at his side, and once he got past all the stables and horse stalls, another building came into view.

The hay barn.

Hudson walked between two fences, with horses on his left and llamas on his right, and made it to the hay barn. Sure enough, around one side, there was a pile of metal. What a normal person didn't know was that not all metals were created equal.

Some could be bent and twisted into spiraled robot legs, and some were meant to hold up tall buildings. He picked through the pieces to find some he could use, but he didn't have the equipment he needed to complete a job such as this one.

He had a friend down in Pasadena he could call, but Hudson left his phone in his pocket and kept looking through the bin of miscellaneous supplies. Wood scraps and metal rods and old horseshoes. Most of this needed to be thrown away, and Hudson realized he was looking at a very small part of what this ranch had to offer.

Scarlett had said her grandfather was a hoarder, and a sigh passed through his body. So he'd help her get the place cleaned up, he'd rebuild the robot, and he'd get those cars fixed. And if he got to spend time with the beautiful Scarlett Adams while he hauled trash and repaired brakes?

Even better.

He went to find her and found her pushing a wheelbarrow across the lawn toward a dumpster. "Hey, can I help you?"

She gave him an icy look and said, "Nope, I'm fine." She picked up a snow shovel and started transferring trash from one container to another.

"I don't think that metal by the hay barn will work," he said. "I need something a little different."

She kept working, barely glancing at him. "I don't have a budget for metal for the mailbox."

"Tell me about the robot. Prime, you called him?" He watched Hound find a patch of shade and flop down.

That got her to stop, and Hudson saw her vulnerability for about half a second before she covered it up again. "My brother named him," she said. "When we were kids, we used to come up here to the ranch in the summer. My grandparents would keep us for a summer, and it was...." She seemed to realize he still stood there, and she cleared her throat.

"It was what?" he asked.

"Wonderful," she said. "And that robot has been there, welcoming everyone to Last Chance Ranch, for over a hundred years." Her chin wobbled slightly. "So I just want you to fix it, because I don't want Prime to die on my watch."

"Scarlett," he said, almost a whisper. "Could I fix it up? Strengthen the joints? Repaint it?"

Their eyes met, and the rest of the world fell away.

Will you go out with me? The words flowed through his mind, but he didn't say them. She barely seemed to like him, though the attraction between them certainly felt electric.

"It's okay if you don't want me to," he finally said, breaking the connection between them. He fell back a step.

"I do," she blurted. "Want you...to fix it up. I just don't want him to disappear."

"He won't," Hudson promised. "And you know, I can help you with all of this." He gestured to the wheelbarrow.

"After you fix the cars," she said, lifting the shovel again. "We need to sell those, because well, as I'm sure you noticed as you went traipsing all over the ranch to find that hay barn, this ranch needs the money."

He suddenly felt like a jerk for demanding sixty percent of the profits.

"And don't worry about your cut," she said. "I know what I'm doing, Mister Flannigan."

He snapped his mouth closed and said, "I need to make a phone call. Then I'll get on those cars."

"Hm." She finished with the last shovel of trash and

promptly turned to go back the way she'd come. He watched her walk away, her hips swaying as she walked.

Hudson swallowed, the temperature suddenly a lot hotter than it had been a moment ago. *Stop it*, he told himself as Scarlett disappeared from view. *Focus on the work.* After all, he didn't want to lose this job he'd just gotten.

So he drew in a deep breath and shelved the idea that he could fix the robot that morning, set aside the fact that he did need to call TJ about the metal he needed, and walked toward the row of cars he'd been shown yesterday.

HUDSON HADN'T SPENT much time inland in the past year, or before that. The breeze that had come off the ocean in Santa Monica kept things cool, even in the summer. But there was no breeze here on the ranch.

Sweat ran down Hudson's face and his back, and he thought he probably looked like he'd been sprayed with a hose. The first car had been an easy fix, with a new set of spark plugs, a fresh oil change, and a replacement timing belt.

The second car needed new tires and new upholstery, as well as a new radiator. He'd made notes on it, but it would take some serious work to get this car in sellable condition.

He currently stood on a step-stool to bend over the

engine of the classic truck, sure his sweat was going to cause an explosion when he tried to start this vehicle. The interior was in perfect condition, if a little dusty, and if this truck had new tires and started, Hudson was sure he could get several thousand dollars for it. Maybe even more.

The 1956 Ford wasn't in immaculate, restored condition. The paint job was probably the original from decades ago, and while there were no rips inside, it wasn't the leather reupholstering he'd seen in some of these classic trucks.

But someone would pay to have this truck, even in its current condition. And if he could get it running, wash it up, and vacuum away all the dust, maybe he could get some cash for the ranch.

He hadn't touched his account in a while, though he had plenty of money from the sale of his shop. He lived off the money he made on his odd jobs, because that money felt authentic. It felt good to be able to work and pay for things with his labor.

He knew his thoughts about the millions in his bank account weren't rational. But they were still his, and he was still working through them.

Scarlett went by with another load of garbage, her face red and glistening. He deliberately kept his head down so he wouldn't ogle her. Now, if he could just figure out what kind of starter he could get at a contemporary automotive store.

He pulled his hands from the engine and wiped them on a rag he'd found in the shed in the corner of the yard.

"Well, I'm done," Scarlett announced, and Hudson almost fell off his step-stool at the sound of her voice. He looked at her to find her bracing her hands against her back and stretching.

His mouth went dry, and he couldn't think of anything to say in response.

"You thirsty?" she asked.

He managed to nod, wondering why he couldn't get his voice to work. He hadn't looked at another woman in such a long time, and he didn't know what to do with all these strange emotions twisting through him.

"Well, come on in," she said. "It's so *hot* today." She walked away, and Hudson jumped off his stool and whistled to his dog.

Hound lifted his head, and Hudson said, "Come on, bud." The dog got to his feet and trotted over, going up the back steps and into the house before Hudson.

A blast of air conditioning hit Hudson in the face, cooling the sweat on his skin and providing sweet relief from the bright sun outside. After walking through a utility room, Hudson entered the kitchen, where Scarlett stood in front of the fridge, moving the door open and closed as if fanning herself.

"Soda?" she asked. "Lemonade? Water?"

"Lemonade," he said, mesmerized by her. "Look, if

you need help around the ranch, I'm more than willing to do it. I have experience with horses."

"Do you? I thought you owned a mechanic shop for twenty years." Scarlett looked at him and then pulled out a case of pink lemonade.

"I did. But I grew up on a horse ranch."

"You don't say." She leaned her hip into the counter and popped the top on a can of soda. The fizzing sound met his ears as he watched her start to drink.

"So I could help out," he said. "You've got a lot of animals here, and sometimes I need a break from the cars."

"How's it going with them?" she asked.

"Good," he said. "I have a list of things I need to get. I'll drive down tonight and get them, and we should be able to get a couple of them fixed tomorrow."

"Really?"

"Yeah. Then I'll wash them, clean out the inside, and we can list them."

"Wow, I'm impressed."

Hudson pulled out a can of pink lemonade and looked at it. "I think maybe I changed my mind. What kind of soda have you got?"

"All kinds," she said. "Adele is kind of a soda freak." She nodded to the fridge. "Help yourself."

"You and Adele," he said, stepping over to the fridge. "You've known each other for a long time?"

"Yeah, we were roommates in college." Scarlett tipped

her head back and drank again, and Hudson couldn't help tracing the curve of her throat with his eyes.

"What was the name of the horse ranch where you grew up?" she asked.

"Thousand Oaks?" he asked, as if she'd know the place. By the blank look on her face, she obviously didn't. So she was just making small talk. She wasn't really interested in him. Bitter disappointment cut through him, along with a healthy dose of foolishness.

"Where is it?"

"It's not too far from here, actually," he said. "Just about twenty minutes further west."

She cocked her head as if she had something more to say, but the front door of the house banged open. A blonde woman wearing a straw hat burst in and said, "Gramps started a fire."

Chapter Five

S carlett blinked, sure she'd heard Adele wrong. "What?"

Hudson didn't wait to get the details. He slammed the fridge closed and strode toward the front door. "Where?" he demanded as he passed her.

"Canine Club," she said, and that got Scarlett to move.

She hurried after the two of them, saying, "What happened?"

"I don't know," Adele said, running after Hudson, who suddenly had the longest legs on the planet. "I came out of my cabin because the goats were bleating like crazy, and I saw the smoke. My car," she called to Hudson. "Get in."

He detoured to the passenger side, and Adele got behind the wheel. Scarlett barely had time to get in the backseat before Adele backed out of the driveway and skidded down the dirt road.

Scarlett's stomach flipped over and over, like a child trying to see if their first batch of pancakes were done yet. She couldn't be the reason a huge wildfire started here. California had so many fires, and what would she do if Last Chance Ranch burned to the ground?

"Please," she whispered. "Please, God, let it be small. Please." She hadn't realized she was speaking out loud until Hudson reached back and curled his fingers around hers.

He didn't say anything, and he didn't need to. His presence was calming in a way Scarlett hadn't anticipated, and as Adele pulled up to the entrance to the Canine Club, a thin trail of smoke lifted into the sky.

"Yes, there's a fire at Last Chance Ranch," Hudson said, removing his hand from hers and getting out of the car. She hadn't even seen him holding his phone to his ear. "I don't know. We're here now, and I'll see. Just wanted to call. Better to be safe than sorry."

Scarlett went through the gate, calling, "Gramps?" She followed the smoke and found him hitting the ground with a towel he'd obviously taken from one of the dog kennels. The building had water spigots on the outside, but they didn't keep the hoses out there because some of their pooches liked to chew them up.

"Gramps, is it burning?" She turned, looking for something to carry water in. She saw a few water bowls and picked them up. "Adele, turn on the water."

She did, and they filled the bowls and hurried over to

Gramps, who kept swatting at the ground. Over and over. "Gramps, back up," Scarlett said, and she poured the water where he'd been hitting. It disappeared so quickly, and more white smoke lifted into the air.

At least it wasn't black, and she turned to get more. She almost ran into Hudson, who had found a big bucket and filled it with water. His biceps strained against the sleeves of his shirt, but Scarlett didn't have time to admire his strength nor the width of his shoulders.

He drenched the grasses where Gramps had been hitting, and he said, "More. Let's make sure it's really out." He nodded back to the building, only a few feet away. "I found another one."

Scarlett went over to it, but there was no way she could lift it. Hudson arrived, handed the empty bucket to Scarlett, and took the nearly full bucket. After several trips back and forth, the ground was good and muddy and the smoke was gone.

A siren filled the air, and Scarlett's plans of an easy afternoon flirting with the handsome new addition to the ranch went up the same way that smoke had. "Why'd you have to call the fire department?" she asked, glaring at Hudson.

"If this was bigger than we could handle—" His dark eyes blazed with fire, and Scarlett held up her hand.

"I know, I know." Scarlett took out her hair and let it flow over her shoulders for a moment. Then she gathered it all together again and put it back in a tight ponytail. "I'm sorry, Hudson. Thank you for all your help." She glanced at Adele, who stood there, still holding a dog bowl.

"Oh, Adele, this is Hudson Flannigan." The sirens grew louder and louder. "Hudson, Adele Woodruff."

"Nice to meet you," he said without extending his hand. "I'll take care of Gramps, yeah?"

Scarlett looked at her grandfather, who'd collapsed into a chair against the side of the building. "Yes, please." She sighed, wondering if the old man had started to lose his mind. The hoarding she could excuse away, due to her grandmother's death. But starting a fire? "See if you can figure out what happened."

She watched Hudson step over to Gramps and touch him gently on his arm before he crouched down and started talking to him. Then she tightened her ponytail, said, "Adele, come with me, okay?" and stepped toward the gate where the fire truck had just pulled behind her best friend's car, blocking it in.

By the time Scarlett finished talking to the firefighters and getting Gramps back to his cabin, exhaustion pounded from the top of her head to the bottom of her feet. "Gramps," she said, sweeping her fingertips along his forehead. "No more trying to move things by yourself, okay?"

"I'm sorry, Scarlett," Gramps said. "I just wanted to help."

"I know." Scarlett pressed her lips to his temple. "It's fine. You don't need to move the fence pieces. I'll get Hudson to do it. Or Sawyer," she said quickly.

Gramps's eyes drifted closed, and he said, "Hadley, tell me how the kids are doing."

Scarlett opened her mouth to say something, but shock kept anything from coming out. Her thoughts tumbled, and then she said, "Gramps, it's Scarlett. I'm Scarlett."

Her phone buzzed in her pocket for the third time since those sirens had come up into the foothills. She wanted to chuck it at the wall and get a new number.

Hadley was her mother, and she suddenly couldn't wait to call her mom and report that Gramps wasn't doing so well. But she stayed with him and talked about her two brothers and her sister. Gramps never asked about Scarlett, and she finally fell silent, sadness permeating the very air in the bedroom.

She got up and tiptoed out to the kitchen, where Adele was making grilled cheese sandwiches. Scarlett sighed as she sat at the kitchen table and pulled out her phone. A groan started somewhere deep inside her when she saw whose call she'd just missed.

"Not Jewel Nightingale." She cradled her head in her hands.

"Who's Jewel Nightingale?" Adele asked, placing a sandwich in front of Scarlett. The scent of browned bread and butter made Scarlett's mouth water.

"She runs Forever Friends," Scarlett said, sitting

upright quickly and dialing her back. The call was only fifteen minutes ago. Maybe Jewel hadn't left for the day yet. But the line just rang and rang, and Scarlett ended up leaving another message and turning to cheese and bread for comfort.

"So that Hudson Flannigan is drop-dead gorgeous," Adele said, joining her at the table.

"Is he?"

"Oh, girl, *please.*" Adele's laughter was entirely too joyful. "I know you, remember? I saw you admiring him."

"When?"

"When he carried those buckets full of water back and forth. *I* was watching him, because dang, the man has muscles, you know?"

"I guess," Scarlett said, taking an overly big bite of her sandwich. Then she'd at least be able to buy herself some time to come up with a reason why she couldn't be interested in Hudson.

The warmth from his hand still lingered in her skin, and she couldn't help flicking a glance at Adele. Her marriage to Vance had been over for years before she'd filed for divorce, and that had taken over three years to become final.

She'd been alone for a long time now, and maybe Hudson stirred something inside her that hadn't been touched in a while. And she didn't have to say any of the things running through her head. Adele knew without Scarlett having to say anything.

"So maybe you'll go out with him," Adele finally said, causing Scarlett to scoff.

"Right," Scarlett said. "Go where? Out to Piggy Paradise for a romantic date?" She giggled, met Adele's eye, and they both started laughing.

When she finally got control of herself, Scarlett shook her head, "No, Adele. My life is this ranch now, and there's nowhere romantic out here."

SCARLETT STOOD with one foot up on the bottom rung of the fence separating her from the llamas. They grazed in the pasture, and everything about the sun setting to her right and the way the crickets had started to chirp was serene.

It was one of the things she'd loved best about coming to the ranch as a child. Even a teenager. The peace this place possessed.

But she felt anything but peaceful as she said, "Mom, he thought I was you." Her voice almost broke, but she contained it. Losing Grams had been hard for everyone, but no one struggled as much as Gramps. Naturally.

Scarlett thought she'd be the most hard-hit by his death, and she couldn't imagine staying on this ranch if he wasn't here.

"He is eighty-one-years-old," her mom said, like that made it okay.

"Should I take him to the doctor?"

"He has no health insurance."

Scarlett didn't either, but she couldn't just let him suffer. If there was something she could do, she should do it. Her parents had insurance, as well as plenty of money. But her mother made no offer to pay for the doctor's visit.

"Any advice?" she asked, wondering why her mother was so unconcerned about this.

"Scarlett, we took him to the doctor last year. He was fine."

"Well, what did they say?" Because he was not fine now. He was trying to move huge eight-by-eight-foot pieces of chainlink fence by himself, starting fires, and forgetting her name.

"They said he was getting older and might get confused from time to time."

"So it's not dementia? Just a memory issue?" Problem was, Scarlett didn't even look all that much like her mother, who'd never worn anything higher than a size six and had dark hair cut into a pixie. Scarlett's auburn locks had come from the slight reddish tint in her father's hair, and her hair fell almost to her waist.

"Probably," her mom said.

"Okay, I have to go," Scarlett said, hanging up a moment later without saying good-bye. Her mother had frustrated her for years, but this took the cake. "Why isn't she concerned?" she wondered aloud to the llama lumbering a little closer to her. She'd named them all, and this brown and white one she'd called Hot Chocolate.

She wasn't particularly enthused about the llamas, as they always wore looks of contempt on their faces. They seemed unpredictable, and she'd read about them online to learn more. They did sometimes have disagreeable dispositions, and she usually kept her distance from them.

Turning to face the horse pasture, she heard the crunch of gravel under someone's feet, and she looked to find Hudson approaching her. "How's Gramps?" he asked, his voice low and deep and sending rumbles through her body.

She reminded herself that the man didn't want to give her his number and that he was only here to earn a buck. Money she didn't have to give him.

"He's okay," she said. "Sleeping."

"What did your mom say?" He joined her at the fence and gazed into the pasture as well.

Scarlett sighed. "She's unconcerned." She cut a glance at Hudson, thinking she might be able to trust him. With enough time, at least. "He called me my mother's name."

"Huh." Hudson let a few seconds of silence go by. "Want me to take him to the doctor when I go down to the automotive shop tomorrow?"

Surprise coursed through her. "You'd do that?"

"Yeah, sure." He put his foot on the bottom rung too. "Did you want to come to the automotive shop with me?"

Her lingering surprise turned into shock. "Why would I want to do that?"

He shrugged and shuffled down the fence a foot or two. "I don't know. You could help me pick out a paint color for the robot, and we could go to lunch...." He stopped talking, and the dusk falling between them seemed to absorb what he'd suggested.

Scarlett had no idea what to say. The signals he put off were so confusing. Maybe she'd been out of the dating game for too long.

"You have a lot of work to do around here," he finally said. "I get it." He knocked twice on the top rung of the fence and started to walk away. "See you later."

The sound of his footsteps had almost faded when she called, "Hudson?"

He stopped, the silhouette of him all she could see. He turned and looked over his shoulder but said nothing.

Feeling brave and drawing that courage all the way into her lungs, she walked toward Hudson. "I can't figure you out," she said when she got close. The sun was almost all the way down now, and she loved the way it eased the earth to sleep.

"Excuse me?" he asked, turning fully now.

She stopped and put her hand on her hip. "First, you wouldn't give me your phone number, and then you're holding my hand in the car, and now lunch?"

Hudson looked away and sighed, and then returned his attention to her. "So you're not ready to date again. I get it. Sorry I asked." He didn't sound sorry, and she wished she could see his face better.

"You don't sound sorry," she said.

"Well, I'm not all that sorry I asked," he said, mirroring her posture by putting his hand on his hip too. "At least now I know you're not interested."

Scarlett opened her mouth to argue—she had an ex-husband, after all—but she said, "I never said I wasn't interested," in a very quiet voice.

Hudson seemed to take forever to take a step forward. "I guess you didn't."

Something bubbled up inside Scarlett, but she had no idea what to call it. Hope, maybe. Excitement, sure.

"So maybe I'll go with you to the automotive shop tomorrow," she said. "Help you pick out that paint."

"Sounds good," he said, tipping his hat at her and turning to go back down the walkway. She hastened to join him, and they barely fit in the space between the two fenced fields. He walked much slower now, and on the third step, he took her hand in his, a simple gesture that sent flutters through her whole chest.

Chapter Six

Hudson wasn't quite sure what he was doing but holding Scarlett's hand felt right. It was almost dark, and he'd have to feel his way back to his cabin. He didn't care. This human connection was more important than almost anything right now, and he couldn't quite articulate how good it felt to hold her hand.

"When I was a little girl, me and my siblings would come out here in the summers," she said, their steps so slow they were barely moving.

"How many siblings?" he asked.

"Two brothers and one sister," she said. "I'm second-oldest."

"I've got three brothers," he said. "I'm the oldest."

"Oh, that explains so much." She gave a light laugh, and he liked how mature it sounded. How flirtatious.

"It does?" he asked, a smile on his face. "How so?"

"You're one of those take-charge kind of men, that's all."

"And...." Hudson wasn't quite sure what to say. "Someone had to put out that fire. Those dog bowls were too small."

Scarlett's laughter flew into the sky, and she bumped into him playfully. "I'm not complaining."

"Hmm," Hudson said as the homestead came into view. "So do you want to call the doctor in the morning? Then we'll know when we can go to town."

"Sure," she said. "Now that I have your phone number I can text you."

"I didn't deliberately withhold my number from you," he said. "And you didn't have to come get Gramps that night. I would've happily brought him back. That was all."

"Which brother were you talking to when I came?"

"Brent," he said. "He's...the only one I speak to at the moment." He couldn't believe he'd told her that, but it was true.

Scarlett didn't immediately demand to know why he wasn't talking to half of his family. Hudson appreciated that, and he liked her even more when she said, "Families are tough. My mother doesn't seem to care that Gramps doesn't know who I am."

"I'm sorry," he said. "Families *are* tough." They passed the three cabins that edged the back of the lawn at the homestead. The scent of curry met his nose, and he wondered what Adele was making for dinner, because it smelled delicious.

"So Gramps is on the end down there. Adele next to him in the middle, and this last one's empty. Is that right?"

"Yeah," she said. "I'm going to put out an ad for more help tonight." She sighed. "I need more people here. I just don't have any way to pay them."

Hudson thought of the amount in his bank account. "Well, I could help out if you need it."

He'd barely finished speaking when she said, "No. That's not necessary. We'll sell the vehicles, and I'm going to get a Forever Friends grant. They called this evening when I was with Gramps."

"That's great," he said. "I need to learn more about them."

"Oh, they do great work with pets and animals," she said. "I've done their Strut Your Mutt events in LA, and they made the city one of the first no-kill cities for dogs." She came alive as she continued to talk about the organization and how she'd toured a few of their facilities.

"And this place could be one," she said. "We have over two hundred acres here, and all the pastures and fields and structures already."

"But no people," he said.

"Right. I need more people. We have some volunteers coming in, but I need people here full-time. And they'll want to get paid and have benefits...." She let her voice trail off, and Hudson squeezed her hand.

"I'm sure you'll make it happen. You're resourceful."

"You think so?"

"Who uses a plastic snow shovel—in California—to scoop trash?" He laughed. "Trust me, Scarlett, you'll be fine." He paused at the back steps, sensing he was going to have to let her go soon. "And I'm willing to help any way you want. I can haul trash. I can fix cars and farm vehicles. I can work with horses and other animals." He faced her and gazed down at her. "You just tell me what to do, and I'll do it."

He didn't mean to sound so desperate, but he feared he did. Scarlett looked up at him, and Hudson had never met such a gorgeous woman.

"So text me in the morning," he said, leaning down quickly and sweeping his lips across her hairline. His cowboy hat prevented him from getting much closer to her, and that was a very good thing.

After all, he'd just met this woman, and her divorce was only four months old. Even if the marriage had been over long before that. Hudson knew that some events carried deep wounds, and he didn't want to push Scarlett too far away before she'd even come too close.

He walked away from her, starting to realize that she needed a few seconds—or even minutes—to process the things he said. Because as he reached the corner of the house, she said, "I'll text you in the morning."

He smiled into the darkness and pulled out his phone so he could turn on the flashlight. He certainly didn't want to trip over something on his way back to his new cabin, and while he'd wandered around this place a lot today, he still didn't know every danger out on these two hundred acres.

"Two hundred acres," he said to the cooling night air. He hadn't even seen half of this ranch, and as he walked, he added, "Please help Scarlett get the grant from Forever Friends."

THE NEXT MORNING, he sat in his truck, waiting for Scarlett and Gramps. She'd texted an hour ago that they had an appointment at ten-thirty, but it was after ten now. They weren't making that appointment, and Scarlett had texted several minutes ago to say Gramps was being difficult and didn't want to go to the doctor.

Hound whined, and Hudson unbuckled his seatbelt to get the dog out so he could take care of his business.

The dog jumped down and started sniffing around while Hudson watched the house. He didn't want to be the take-charge kind of guy and go see if she needed help. Or did he? He still wasn't sure if that was a good thing or not.

Hound finished and jumped back into the truck just as Scarlett came around the back of the house, Gramps on her arm. Hudson hurried forward to help her, and he steadied Gramps on the uneven lawn. He helped the older man into the truck, telling Hound to get in the back, and held the door for Scarlett too.

Once everyone was in, he said, "Are you going to direct me there?" he asked, backing out of the driveway.

"Yes," Scarlett said, a definite clip to her voice. The tension in the truck could've been cut with a butter knife, and Hound leaned his head over the seat and put it between Scarlett and her grandfather.

"I'm sorry," Gramps said. "I just don't like doctors." He reached up to pat Hound's head, and the golden retriever seemed to be in bliss. Hudson turned his head away from them as he smiled, grateful once more for his dog.

"You know, Hound's great company," he said. "He was all I had left after my marriage ended."

"He's a good dog," Gramps said.

"I'm sure he'd love to stay with you sometime," Hudson said. "I bet they'd let you take him into the doctor's office too."

"You think so?" Scarlett asked, and Hudson looked at her.

"I have a service animal vest in the back," he said, hoping she wouldn't ask him why in front of Gramps. "They usually don't ask any questions when he wears that."

She directed him left and right and they pulled up to the office only a few minutes late. Hudson busied himself with putting the vest on Hound and attached a leash to his collar. Then he handed the leash to Gramps, and said, "Go on, Hound."

Scarlett linked her arm through Gramps's, and they went into the office together. A few minutes later, she texted with a simple *Thank you, Hudson.*

He waited in the shade, playing a game on his phone, and when Scarlett came out of the building with Gramps, it was clear she'd been crying. He jumped to his feet and tucked his phone in his back pocket.

"Hey," he said, drawing her into a hug. He was somewhat surprised she let him, but she did, and she held onto him for a few seconds. Then she pulled away and swiped at her face.

"Let's go to lunch," she said in a falsely bright voice. "Gramps says he's tired, and I said we could drive him and Hound back to the ranch first." Their eyes met, and so much was said in just a moment. No words.

Hudson liked that, and he nodded before helping everyone up into the truck. It was twenty minutes back to the ranch, but he didn't care. Once Gramps was settled in his recliner, Hound on the floor at his feet, Hudson went back to the truck with Scarlett, glad for air conditioning.

"This is a nice truck," she said as she buckled her seatbelt.

"I bought it when I sold the shop," he said. "The camper shell too. That's where I've lived for the past year."

Scarlett turned toward him. "Really?"

"It's not bad," he said. "It has a shower and a two-burner stove. A microwave. A bed. I even have a TV." Hudson made it sound better than it was. "I don't mind a small house. It's the...loneliness that was hard to contend with."

"Ah, loneliness. We're well-acquainted."

Hudson smiled and asked, "Where do you want to go to lunch?"

"There's a great Mexican place on Palm Street," she said.

"I think I know it," he said, making a turn as they came out of the canyon.

She ran her fingers through her hair and adjusted her sunglasses. "I have a few people who've already applied for jobs around the ranch," she said. "I was wondering if you'd help me with the interviews. I've been at Last Chance for a couple of weeks, but you grew up on a horse ranch."

"Sure," he said. "Just tell me when."

"I haven't set any of them up yet," she said. "But I'd like to start as soon as possible. When Forever Friends come to the ranch, I'm going to need to show them that I have the manpower to take on more animals."

"You already have over one hundred," he said. "How many do you think you can handle?"

"I have no idea." She sighed and combed through her hair again. He really wanted to do that, maybe right before he kissed her. He tamed his fantasies and made another turn, the Mexican restaurant coming into view further down the road.

"There's probably regulations for things like that," he said.

"Probably." A moment later, she pulled out her phone and started tapping.

He parked and looked at her. "You're looking it up right now, aren't you?"

Her hazel eyes—more green than brown—met his, and the guilt was right there in them. "Maybe." She pushed her phone against her chest, and Hudson maybe let his gaze linger there for a moment too long.

Embarrassed, he yanked his attention away and out the front windshield. "Should we go in?"

"Yes." She got out of the truck, and he met her at the front of it. "I couldn't find anything about how many animals per acre I can have."

Hudson chuckled and said, "Well, no one can ever say you're not thorough."

She laughed too, and Hudson slipped his hand into hers as they went inside, his nerves firing in such a way to remind him that he was on a date. His first date in over a decade.

Could it be his last first date?

He shook the thought out of his head as they walked to their table. He'd always thought a little too far ahead, and he was determined not to do that here.

Scarlett was beautiful, yes. Capable, definitely.

Strong-willed and smart. She wouldn't be rushed, and Hudson didn't even want to rush her.

Now that he was older, he knew how to savor every moment, and that was what he wanted to do with Scarlett Adams. And if he could enjoy chips and salsa at the same time? Well, that was a win-win in Hudson's book.

Chapter Seven

E vening once again found Scarlett visiting with the animals as the sun went down. This time, it was the potbellied pigs, which was fine. Sure, they smelled a little worse than the llamas or the horses, but they also seemed a bit more joyful.

She smiled at the two who'd flopped on the ground a few feet from her, and said, "And then we went to the automotive store and got all the parts he needed for a couple of the cars in the yard. He's going to fix those up and sell them."

She'd told them all about the date at Beanie's, and how charming Hudson could be. He'd also shared several personal things with her, and she appreciated his maturity and wisdom. He hadn't expounded on why he didn't talk to two of his brothers, and he didn't seem keen on driving the twenty minutes to his family's horse ranch.

There was definitely a story there, but she didn't want to press him for details. He'd share when he was ready—same as her. She didn't need him asking her all kinds of questions she didn't want to answer.

"Then we went to his buddy's scrap metal facility, and we got all the pieces he needs to fix Prime." She fell silent again, more memories of her childhood filtering through her mind. She loved that robot, and she loved this ranch, and as she stood there, she realized she'd do whatever she could to preserve it.

Why? ran through her mind, and she didn't have an answer. She had no children to pass the ranch to, and none of her siblings seemed all that interested in even visiting Last Chance Ranch. But she couldn't just let the place go. What would happen to all the animals?

But the real question was: What would happen to her?

"Anyway, I have a couple of interviews with people tomorrow," she said. "I'm going to get someone dedicated to you guys. To Piggy Paradise." Right now, she fed them and Adele cleaned out their stalls every so often. Since it was summer, the pigs didn't really live inside all that much, but she knew there was more someone could be doing for them. It wasn't just enough to keep them alive.

She left them there before dusk started to settle, and her phone rang. Her heart thumped, and her mind screamed at her to get it because it could be Jewel Nightingale.

Sure enough, it was, and Scarlett paused on the north

side of the hay barn, apparently a conversation with Jewel too hard to do while walking. "Hello?" she asked as if she didn't know who was on the other end of the line.

"Scarlett," Jewel said like they were long-lost friends who hadn't seen each other in years. "I'm so glad I got you this time."

"Yeah," Scarlett said with a laugh. "We've been playing phone tag a little."

"Just a little. Listen." She drew in a deep breath. "I'm intrigued by your ranch, and I want to come see it."

"Really?" Scarlett pressed her eyes closed and wished she could suck that word back into her throat. "I mean—"

"I just need a couple of weeks to get my team together. A couple of them are on vacation. Then we'll come up and see what you've got. We always want to partner with local farms and ranches to help as many animals as possible. I'm sure you know we're close to having California be a no-kill *state* for dogs, and we couldn't do it without farms like yours."

"Great," Scarlett said. "When can you come?"

"Ah." She exhaled and sighed. "Let me call you back on that, okay? I'm not in the office right now, and I need to put together a team. I just wanted to touch base and find out what kind of animals you have."

"Let's see," Scarlett said. "I've got horses, llamas, and potbellied pigs. I've got dogs and cats and goats. I've got a couple of sheep and some cattle."

"No birds?"

"No birds." She wanted to add *thank goodness*, because birds seriously freaked her out. But she bit back the words. Someone like Jewel probably wouldn't appreciate it, as she ran an organization committed to saving all animals, including birds.

"What kind of buildings do you have?" she asked next, and Scarlett realized how woefully unprepared she was for Forever Friends to come visit Last Chance Ranch.

Her mind spun back to the time she'd toured one of their facilities in Utah. "Let's see, we've got barns and outdoor enclosures for the bigger animals. Stalls for the horses and cows for when it rains. Same for the pigs, llamas, and goats. The dogs and cats have an indoor facility with separate enclosures. They have air conditioning."

"Any cabins or administration buildings?"

"We have sixteen cabins," she said. "The homestead. And a group of buildings that could probably be administration buildings, but they're empty right now."

"I think I know your ranch," Jewel said next, her voice thoughtful. "I think we've been up there before."

Scarlett couldn't tell if that was a good thing or not. All she could say was, "Oh."

Something scratched on Jewel's end of the line and she said something in a muffled voice, obviously not to Scarlett. "Okay," she said, distracted now. "I have to go, but I'll call you back in a couple of days to set up a date, okay?"

"Okay," Scarlett said, and the call ended.

She turned in a full circle, finally settling on the idea to walk straight north to the buildings she hadn't paid much attention to. She hadn't given them a second thought, because the buildings were empty, and she had plenty of other priorities at the ranch.

"I need a couple of weeks, at least," she whispered. "Okay, Lord? If I have a couple of weeks, I can get all the trash off the ranch, and Jewel won't have to know what this place looked like when I showed up."

Pure exhaustion kept her from going into the buildings. She wasn't afraid, exactly, but she also wasn't stupid, and she couldn't remember what was inside the buildings. She needed to come back when she was fresh, with a notebook and a pen so she could take notes of what the facilities were like and what they needed to be presentable to Jewel and her team.

Just the word *team* sent a flicker of fear through her. Not only would she have to impress Jewel, but others as well.

Oh, she had so much work to do. Tomorrow. She would start tomorrow.

TOMORROW CAME, and so did the first man she was interviewing. "His name is Carson Chatworth," she said, reading off her phone. "He said he's worked on a Montana ranch for his whole life."

Adele sat on her right and Hudson on her left. Scarlett was still nervous. She hadn't ever interviewed or hired someone before. Her assistant at the marketing firm had been appointed to her, and she was used to trying to impress her bosses not be impressed by anyone.

She adjusted the notebook in front of her, but honestly, if this Carson guy walked in and didn't creep her out, Scarlett would hire him.

She'd gone through one of the buildings that morning, and it was really just like Gramps's cabin. She supposed it could be used for a center for volunteers. Training sessions. Check-ins. That kind of thing. Yes, she'd also spent a couple of hours on the Forever Friends website last night, making notes of all the things they did, and writing down facilities they needed to do them.

And Last Chance Ranch would definitely need a place to handle volunteers. And adoptions. And a veterinary clinic.

But this guy—Carson—wasn't a vet.

A knock sounded on the door, and Scarlett practically threw her chair into the wall behind her as she stood up. "I'll get it." She left Hudson and Adele at the kitchen table and went to answer the door.

Carson Chatworth stood on the porch, and he certainly looked like a cowboy. Big, black hat. Blue checkered shirt. Jeans. Boots. He could show up on a

Hollywood set right now and get every western role available.

With those stormy gray eyes and neatly trimmed beard, he was quite handsome. "Hello," he said, flashing a dazzling smile at her. "I'm Carson Chatworth." He extended his hand for her to shake, and she pumped it a couple of times, noting that there were no butterflies when he touched her the way there were when Hudson did.

"Come on in," she said. "I'm Scarlett Adams. I've got my associates with me today." She pointed to Hudson. "Hudson Flannigan. And Adele Woodruff."

"Hello," he said, his smile perfectly in place. He shook Hudson's hand and then Adele's while Scarlett took her chair between them.

"So," Scarlett said with an exhale. "You worked a ranch in Montana?"

"I owned the ranch," he said, and Adele scoffed to her right. Scarlett looked at her and she folded her arms.

So she didn't like this guy. Scarlett wondered why not. He was perfect, and if he'd owned a ranch, Scarlett wanted him here for more than his expertise with horses.

"Why don't you own it now?" Hudson asked, his voice perfectly even.

"I had to sell it," he said. "And I'm looking for a new place to be."

Hudson shifted, and Scarlett realized that he understood Carson's statement, probably on a deeper level than she knew. She thought of his truck and camper shell, which she still hadn't gotten a tour of, despite his promise to do so.

"Mostly horses?" Scarlett asked.

"Horses, cattle, whatever," he said. "I can clean stalls and do ranch maintenance. I can fix fences, and feed animals, and assess their needs. I know agriculture issues and have managed the farming aspect on a working cattle ranch."

"Finances?" Scarlett asked, scribbling the things he'd said.

"I had an accountant," he said. "But I knew what was going on. We met regularly, and I could definitely do that too." He flashed another smile. "Whatever you need."

Scarlett needed a lot, but she didn't need to consult with Hudson and Adele on this guy. "Great." She reached across the table and shook his hand again. "You're hired. Adele, will you take him over to the Community and let him pick out a cabin?"

Adele kicked her under the table, causing Scarlett to look at her. "What?"

Adele gave one quick shake of her head, but Scarlett had another interview in fifteen minutes. And she wanted Hudson there. Adele had been here for moral support. Carson stood up and Scarlett did too.

"Adele will take you over," she said. "I'm assuming you need somewhere to live? We have cabins on-site, and that's part of your pay."

"Sounds great," he said, glancing at Adele.

Adele glared at Scarlett as she led the way to the front door, finally tearing her gaze when she had to leave the house.

"What's with her?" Hudson asked, and Scarlett shook her head.

"I don't know. She probably didn't like his shirt or something." She'd find out later, because there had definitely been something between Carson and Adele.

Just like there was between Scarlett and Hudson, as the fireworks popped through her when he leaned closer and asked, "Want to order pizza tonight and hang out with me and Hound?"

Chapter Eight

Hudson felt like he'd fallen into a dream. No, his house wasn't very big, but he'd never cared about the mansion overlooking the ocean the way Jan had. In fact, he didn't even own this cabin, and that was just fine with him.

He was tired at the end of the night, because he worked. That felt good. He'd been loaning Hound to Gramps to help him sleep, but he had the dog with him that night as he waited for the pizza to arrive.

Oh, and Scarlett. He was waiting for her to arrive too.

He moved the stack of napkins slightly, thinking both should be here already. Just then, he heard her voice say, "No, I got it. Thanks."

In the next moment, Scarlett opened the door and said, "Knock, knock." She came in carrying the two boxes of pizza, and Hudson sprang forward.

"Let me take them."

But she maneuvered past him, that sexy smile on her face. "I got it."

Hudson went out on the porch to pay for the food, but the guy was already back in his car, backing back onto the dirt road. "Did you pay him?"

"Yep."

"Scarlett." Hudson went back inside the cabin and closed the door. "You didn't need to pay him."

"Oh, I have an account with Pie Squared. It's fine."

Hudson made a mental note of that, and next time he ran down to town, he'd be settling that account. He knew he had more money than Scarlett did, but he pushed his annoyance down. He could take care of the bill later, and she was here now.

"So I got a meat lovers," he said. "Because that's what I like. And for you...." He opened the top box and saw the pepperoni, sausage, and ham and promptly closed the lid. The scent of meat and marinara made his mouth water.

"For you...let's see. What's your favorite kind of pizza?"

"Is this a magic trick?" Her eyes glittered at him, and he sure liked this game they were playing.

"Maybe," he said, switching the order of the boxes so the second one was on top. "Depends on if you answer with what I ordered."

"Chicken Alfredo," she said, and Hudson actually froze.

"Really?" he asked, lifting the lid. "I mean, I figured you'd like white sauce better than red, but...really?" He looked down at the cheesy chicken Alfredo pizza. It had red and green onions, along with big chunks of chicken. It actually looked good, but it was no meat lovers.

"No," she said, laughing. Her long hair swung as she shook her head. "The guy read me the order outside." She took a piece of the chicken Alfredo anyway and plopped it onto a paper plate.

Foolishness hit Hudson, but he didn't show it. He set the boxes side by side on the counter and took three pieces of his precious meat lovers for himself. "What is your favorite pizza?"

"You were close," she said. "I don't really like marinara. But I definitely like chicken barbecue. Or the chicken bacon ranch is divine."

"So I was half right." He watched her take a bite of her pizza, and the desire to kiss her shot through the roof.

"Mm." She licked her lips and reached for a napkin. After swallowing she added, "Yeah, half right. And this is great. Really."

She twisted, got another piece of pizza, and went into the living room. He sat beside where she perched on the couch, and they ate in companionable silence for a moment. Then she asked, "Can I feed Hound?"

"He'll drool all over if you don't." Hudson held out a piece of sausage and Hound took it with the softest lips.

Scarlett fed him a chunk of chicken and then cut

Hudson a look out of the corner of her eye. "What do you think I should assign Carson to do?"

Hudson exhaled like the decision was hard. "He's a career cowboy," he said. "He could do anything." He didn't want to tell Scarlett what to do. It was her ranch.

"Maybe I should have him coach me," she mused, her gaze on something only she could see.

"He'd be great with any of the animals," Hudson said. "And you've got me for the horses, and Sawyer does the lessons already. He's mainly over farming, so you could turn over the cattle to Carson. He did come from a cattle ranch."

"I'm going to give him the llamas and pigs too," Scarlett said. "That'll free me up to do other things."

"What other things?"

"Jewel called me back the other night," she said. "Last night. Was it just last night?" She shook her head. "I swear, the days out here mesh together."

That they did. Ranch life had a way of doing that, because there were no days off. Hudson found his shop had operated in much the same way. He could work seven days a week and still never be caught up.

"Anyway." Scarlett blew out her breath. "Jewel called, and she's putting together a team to come see the ranch. I want it to be ready when she comes."

"And by ready, you mean...."

"No trash," she said. "That dumpster has to be gone.

Gramps's cabin has to be spotless. All the buildings over there by Feline Frenzy? Those have to be gone through, repaired, cleaned, and be ready for Jewel's inspection."

"Feline Frenzy?" Hudson asked, a laugh immediately following.

"Yes," Scarlett said, giving him a glare that really held no power behind it. Now Adele. She could glare a man's face off, and Hudson was actually surprised Carson still had his eyes, nose, and mouth.

"I named all the areas here at the ranch."

"Of course," Hudson said like that was the most natural thing in the world.

"I got the idea from Forever Friends," she said. "Jewel will love it. Oh!" She put her empty paper plate down. "So I need signs made for each of the areas. How good are you with wood?"

"Wood?" he repeated.

"Yeah." She reached over and took his plate—not empty—and set it next to hers on the table in front of them. "I mean, you work magic with metal with your hands." She took both of his in hers and ran her fingers down his.

Sparks erupted through Hudson, and he found it quite difficult to breathe. He marveled at how she could affect him so strongly when he'd been in love before, been married before, been devastated before.

Was he really going to go through all of that again?

For her? The question ran through his mind, being chased by the answer.

Oh, yeah.

For Scarlett Adams, Hudson was willing to get his heart broken again.

"You have such big hands," she said, her voice almost a whisper. "Strong. Capable." She turned them over like she'd read his palms. "Surely you can make a sign for each of the animal habitats."

She looked up at him through her eyelashes, and Hudson's imagination went wild. He blinked, trying to focus on the reality in front of him.

"I suppose I can make a sign," he said. "You want it painted or something?" The words scratched his dry throat, and he focused on her lips as they curved upward.

She looked at his hands again, still holding them as if they were precious. "Surprise me, okay?"

Hudson chuckled and gently withdrew one of his hands from her, curling his fingers of his other one around hers. "Scarlett, I don't think you're surprise-able."

"Surprise-able? That's not a word."

He leaned back into the couch, a smile on his face and a sigh on his lips. "It is tonight."

She joined him, but she definitely carried a pout in her voice when she asked, "You think I can't be surprised?"

"I think you know exactly what you want those signs to look like, and you'd best just open your phone and show me so I don't waste my time."

Scarlett's hand slipped out of his, and Hudson regretted his words. He opened his eyes and prepared to apologize only to find her swiping on her phone. She held it up for him, and he examined the bright, colorful signs she'd obviously found on a crafting website.

"May I?" He reached for the phone and took it from her to get a closer look. The letters were raised, which meant they'd been carved somehow. Then painted. "You have wood for this?"

"There's a bunch of wood way out in the corner of the ranch," she said. "I found it when I first got here. We'll take the four-wheeler in the morning, if you'd like." She folded her arms. "And I'd like your help going through the buildings too."

He looked at the signs again, thinking an old, neglected wood pile would not yield them the supplies he needed to make signs look like the ones she wanted. He handed her phone back and said, "I can make the signs. Do you have tools?"

"We should talk to Sawyer."

"I can help with the buildings," he said, though what he really wanted to ask was when he was supposed to fix those cars.

She curled into his side, and he lifted his arm around her, finding her adorable and attractive at a new level. "I'll just steal you away from the cars in the morning," she said as if she'd read his mind.

"Because you need those out of the yard before Jewel comes too, right?" He didn't need to ask.

"Right," she said.

He sighed. "You really drive a hard bargain, Scarlett," he said, brushing his lips against her temple.

"Yes, well, I'm worth it," she said, a giggle following. Hudson didn't contradict her, because he had the distinct feeling that she was indeed worth the effort.

"I have a question for you," he said, and she stiffened for a moment.

"Yeah?"

"Do you know of a church I can attend on Sunday?"

"Yeah, sure," she said. "There's a little red brick church a block or two from the road that leads up here. Gramps has been going there for decades."

Hudson nodded. "Do you go to church, Scarlett?" He wasn't sure why he was asking. Jan hadn't been particularly religious. Hudson either, for that matter. Sure, he believed in God, and he went to church on occasion. But if Jan wanted to go to the beach, or there was a car to be fixed, Hudson could've just as easily chosen those tasks on the Sabbath.

At least until he'd learned about Jan's infidelity. Then he'd really turned to the Lord, and He'd become Hudson's only friend over the past year. Well, besides Hound.

"Sometimes," she said. "I didn't go in the city much. Vance—that was my husband—didn't care much for religious things."

Hudson let his thoughts drift and settle. Then he said, "My brother—one of the ones I don't talk to—is a minister. Jude and I never really saw eye-to-eye about anything. Even growing up, he was always so much better than me."

"Pastor Williams is great," Scarlett said. "I mean, I've only been once since moving here, but Gramps likes him. I don't think he'd judge you."

"Jude doesn't judge," Hudson said, trying to find the right word for how his brother acted.

"I didn't mean to say he did," Scarlett said. "I just—" She cut off, and Hudson felt her nervousness coursing through him.

"It's fine," he said. "I'm not offended."

She relaxed, and he found the word he'd been searching for. "Jude is condescending. Holier-than-thou. Pretentious." So he'd found a lot of words for Jude.

Hudson wasn't surprised at Jude's attitude, actually. His father's was almost identical, and Jude had never fallen far from the Flannigan tree.

"So you didn't get along because he was religious and you sort of weren't?" she asked.

"No, he thought all mechanics were crooks. Couldn't believe that was what I'd choose to do, and he bragged about how he hadn't taken his car in for anything in years. Changed his own oil and everything." Hudson rolled his eyes, though he didn't particularly enjoy having these dark feelings about his own brother.

"I'm sorry," she said, and Hudson once again felt at

peace with his life choices. Not everyone acted the way his father and Jude did, and Hudson had never ripped anyone off. He got paid to fix cars—there wasn't anything wrong with that.

And for the first time in a year, Hudson felt like there wasn't anything wrong with his life at all.

Chapter Nine

Scarlett caught the scent of cinnamon and yeast as she knocked on Adele's door. "Adele," she called through the wood. "Can I come in?"

A moment later, the door opened two inches to reveal a sliver of her best friend's face. "No. I'm busy."

"Busy?" Scarlett stretched up on her tiptoes to try to see over Adele's head. "Did you make cinnamon rolls?"

Adele opened the door further and squeezed out onto the porch with Scarlett. "I don't want to talk about it. You said I'd have my privacy out here."

"From cinnamon rolls?" Scarlett looked down at Adele. "You're acting really weird. Secret baking and what was with all that glaring at Carson the other day?" In fact, Adele had made herself very scarce around the homestead since then too. "And you still won't tell me what you're plotting with the goats."

Scarlett folded her arms and waited for Adele to start talking. When she didn't, Scarlett sighed like she was being difficult on purpose, because she was. Adele had always been more of a planner than Scarlett. She didn't reveal things until she was sure they would work, and she usually had most of the details already worked out.

She lifted her chin and said, "I'm willing to tell you two things. Name them."

Scarlett grinned at her. "One: Carson."

Adele rolled her eyes. "Oh, I met him in town the day before he came up for the interview. He was a real jerk, and I was shocked to see him show up here. That's all."

"Met him in town? You didn't mention that."

"Yeah, well, nothing worth mentioning." Adele crossed her arms too, and her voice pitched up slightly.

"You didn't think an incredibly hot man was worth mentioning?"

"Not all of them are," Adele said. "Besides, he doesn't need this job."

"How do you know that? He applied."

"Yeah, because he's homesick and bored." She shook her head. "He sold that ranch in Montana because oil was discovered on it. He has plenty of money."

Understanding flooded Scarlett. "Oh, so you hate him on principle."

"That's right," Adele said, her eyes widening. "I hate him on principle."

Scarlett didn't want to be unsupportive. Adele had

been there through every step of her separation and divorce. They'd always been there for each other. She drew her friend into a hug and said, "I'm sorry it still hurts."

Adele melted into her and her shoulders shook for only a moment. "I hate that it still hurts." She pulled away and wiped her face. "I hate that he still gets to make me feel like this."

"It gets better," Scarlett said. "I mean, I know you hate it when I say that, but it's true."

Adele nodded and tucked her hair behind her ear, where it fell right back out again. "What's the second thing?"

Scarlett looked at the closed front door and back to the homestead, though she couldn't see the Goat Grounds from here. "Goats," she said.

Adele drew herself up to her full height, which was a couple of inches taller than Scarlett. "Fine, but I don't have all the details worked out yet, so keep that in mind."

"It's in mind."

"Goat yoga." She said each word individually, with a big space between them.

"Goat yoga?" Scarlett asked, a laugh immediately coming out. When Adele didn't even smile, she cut the sound off. "Really, Adele?"

"Really, Scarlett. People are doing all kinds of alternative exercise these days, and yoga is huge. Hot yoga. Beach yoga. And we could do goat yoga. I'm a trained yoga instructor, and we have the facilities. They've been doing it down South for a year or so—I saw it on TV a couple of months back—and I've been training the baby goats."

"Baby goats?"

"Well, you can't have a fifty-pound adult goat jumping on people."

"The goats jump on people?" Scarlett couldn't believe what she was hearing. "Adele...."

"No, really." She held up her hand. "I have a whole folder of information on it. The babies only weigh about fifteen pounds or so, and they are so smart. I've been training them with graham crackers, and they let me pick them up. They jump on my back when I'm doing my poses. They're awesome. And—*and*." She took a deep breath. "We could charge $25 per person for an hour of yoga with the goats. Put up to thirty people in that enclosure we've got out there next to the pens. I've been leveling it and with straw down, it's perfect. The babies are used to being in there, and if we could get the mats, we'd be set to go. Sort of."

Scarlett needed some time to absorb everything she'd said, not to mention how much thirty yoga mats would cost. Instead, she seized on, "Sort of?"

"Well, I need someone to help me run the program. Maybe a couple of people."

"To do what?"

"While I'm teaching yoga, I'd need at least one person

to tend to the goats. Make sure they jump up on every person, circle them through the people. Stuff like that."

Scarlett looked at her, glee coursing through her. "You know who you can have, right?"

Adele was a smart woman, and she immediately started shaking her head. "No. Scarlett, come on. Give me Hudson."

Scarlett started laughing. "No way. I've already got him making signs. Not only that, but I just assigned him to Horse Heaven, and he still has to fix all those cars." She pushed her flyaways back and sighed. "Jewel Nightingale called a couple of nights ago, and this place has to be *perfect* when she comes. Hudson's helping me with all of that."

"Oh, I bet he is." Adele grinned and lifted her eyebrows.

Scarlett shrugged. "And maybe I like him a little bit." More than a little bit, but Scarlett didn't want to quantify it, even to herself.

"I thought we weren't doing boyfriends on the ranch."

"Oh, we're not," Scarlett said. "I mean, you hate Carson. So you're safe. *We* aren't doing anything." She moved down the steps, her two questions satisfied. "Anyway, I stopped by to ask you if you'd talk to Carson about taking over in LlamaLand and Piggy Paradise." At the bottom of the stairs, she turned back and smiled up at her friend. "And now goat yoga too. It sounds like it could really bring in some cash."

"Yeah, about that." Adele skipped down the steps. "I, uh, want half the money. The other half can go to the ranch."

Scarlett wasn't a math genius, but she knew a twenty-five-dollar fee times thirty people was almost eight hundred dollars per session.

"How often are we doing goat yoga?" she asked.

"I was thinking every morning and every evening," she said. "We're not that far up the canyon, and we might get people who come every day."

"Not for twenty-five dollars a class," Scarlett said.

"So we offer them a monthly fee, the way a gym membership does."

"I'm sure you have all those details in your folder," Scarlett said.

"I'm still working on it," Adele said.

"Talk to Carson," Scarlett said. "And I'd love to see this goat yoga going before Jewel comes out to the ranch. Let's talk again tonight, and I want to see times for the sessions. I'll try to schedule her to come while one is running."

"Thanks, Scarlett. And one more thing."

Scarlett turned back, her impatience nearly getting the best of her. "Yeah?"

"Could you ask Hudson about fixing my car? It has a starter problem."

She grinned and nodded. "That's an easy one. I'll talk

to him." She started across the lawn again, late for yet another interview.

THE FOLLOWING WEEK, Scarlett sat at the dining room table with her cup of chamomile tea, enjoying a lazy start to yet another Friday. She and Hudson had taken Gramps to church on Sunday, and it had been so peaceful sitting on the bench and listening to the pastor talk about forgiveness.

With Hudson's help, she'd finished the clean-up of Gramps's cabin. He was out there making repairs, and then they'd repaint and put down new floors to complete the renovation. They'd gone through all of the buildings and Hudson had literally worked late into the night to fix cracks, re-plaster walls, and replace broken windows.

Scarlett had never considered herself a great painter, but she'd done six rooms in the past four days, and wow, her back was tired. So tired.

Jewel had called and scheduled an appointment for next Monday, so she still had ten days to get the ranch into tip-top shape. Adele and Carson's first goat yoga class was scheduled for next Saturday morning, and they'd been spending a lot of time together out in the Goat Grounds, and it turned out that Adele had skills in web design too.

There was still plenty to do around the ranch, but Scarlett just wanted to enjoy her tea. She lifted her cup at the same time someone pounded on the front door, causing her to startle and spill hot liquid on the back of her hand.

Before she could answer, Hudson burst in. "I just sold another car." He wore a look of utter triumph on his face, and he crossed the room to her in three long strides and threw a wad of cash on the table.

She gaped at it. "Holy cow, Hudson." She jumped up, the burn from her tea suddenly unimportant. The bills in her hand felt like relief, and she counted out two thousand dollars. "Which car?"

"That little blue sedan. All it needed was the spark plugs and the belt, remember? A hundred-dollar fix."

"Excellent profit," she said, counting out twelve hundred dollars with fifties and twenties. She held it out to him, finding him so desirable when he was happy.

"Nope," he said. "That's your cut."

She looked at the money and back at him. "You're kidding."

"I'm not." He'd sold another car a couple of days ago, but it hadn't fetched nearly as much. "And I have that 1956 Ford down at the intersection, along with the white car I finished yesterday. I've already had three calls about that truck." He looked at his phone as it chimed. "We're going to bring in a lot of money for that truck, I'm telling you."

Scarlett finally felt like the sky was lifting, like she could make this ranch into something wonderful and worthwhile. She squealed and danced over to Hudson, throwing her arms around him. "Thank you, Hudson."

He held her tight, and the moment sobered as she realized what she'd done. She pulled back but didn't remove herself from the safety and thrill of his arms. She gazed up at him, the connection that existed between them strengthening and solidifying as the seconds ticked past.

"Scarlett," he whispered, his gaze dropping to her mouth. She wasn't so new to relationships that she didn't know what he was asking when he said her name.

She had to admit she'd been thinking about him a lot. They worked together all day, and held hands, and laughed. If she cooked, which she hardly ever did, he ate with her, or they ordered food and stole a few minutes of relaxation while they ate together.

She let her eyes drift closed, her silent permission for him to go ahead and kiss her now. She detected a slight movement in him before the back door crashed open.

Scarlett yelped and jumped back, pressing one hand over her heart as she took in the sight of Adele standing there, the same pure joy on her face.

"Goat yoga just sold out," she said.

Scarlett still had her hand on Hudson's waist, and she hurried to pull it back to her side. "Next Saturday just sold out? Didn't you just open registration this morning?"

"An hour ago." Adele laughed as she came forward. "And Saturday evening is sold out. And Monday morning, and *every* morning this month!" She grabbed onto Scarlett's hands and they bounced up and down as the realization of what she'd said sunk into Scarlett's mind.

Their laughter mixed together, and it wasn't until Carson entered the house and cleared his throat that Adele sobered.

"So we'd like to go over a few logistics," Adele said, pure professionalism in her voice now. "Do you have a few minutes?" She threw a glance at Hudson.

Scarlett did too, the moment between them gone but still heated. "Yeah, sure," she said. "Hudson and I can chat later."

All she could hope for was that Hudson would know that by "chat," Scarlett really meant "kiss."

He nodded his head, touched the brim of his cowboy hat in a salute, and moved effortlessly out the front door, leaving Scarlett to discuss goat yoga with Adele and Carson, who definitely had their own kind of charge between them.

Chapter Ten

Hudson sat with Scarlett, Adele, and Gramps in church, having listened to the two women chatter about the upcoming goat yoga class for the quick drive down the canyon. And yesterday. And most of Friday.

He wasn't tired of it, just a little frustrated that goats had stolen his time with Scarlett. Baby goats. Adele and Scarlett had gone to town and bought a bunch of yoga mats with the cash he'd given her from the sale of the cars. She'd also bought him new wood for the signs, and the amount of work that loomed before him threatened to overwhelm him.

He appreciated Sunday, because he didn't have to worry about work. About paying bills. About anything. Inside the church where they sat, he wasn't troubled with worldly things. He refused to let them disturb his day of rest.

Scarlett scooted closer to him on the bench and said, "Adele is cooking after church today. She wants to know if you'd come so there's a buffer between her and Carson."

Hudson leaned down, his mouth dangerously close to Scarlett's earlobe. "Can she cook?" He seemed to remember smelling some amazing scents a few times as he passed Adele's cabin in the evenings.

"Oh, yeah," Scarlett said.

"Then sure." He kept his head bent toward her. "But why does she need a buffer between her and Carson? Why doesn't she just not invite him?"

"She was raised in the South," Scarlett said as if that explained everything.

"Is she barbecuing after church?" Because that would change everything.

"She didn't say." Scarlett nodded toward the pulpit, where the pastor had just moved to stand behind.

Hudson slid his hand into Scarlett's, thrilled that she didn't pull away. He shouldn't be surprised. She'd practically kissed him a couple of days ago, and her initial frosty demeanor had vanished completely.

He listened to Pastor Williams talk about embracing change without fear, wondering if God had spoken directly to the preacher about what Hudson needed to hear most. He enjoyed feeling like his life had purpose. That he could do better tomorrow than he had today. That though he was now employed at Last Chance Ranch, he could have multiple chances to repent and do better.

The hour passed quickly, and when he stood to sing the final hymn, he appreciated the opportunity to be where he was. He'd been all over the state in the past year, and it seemed a touch ironic that he'd come back to these foothills. His family's ranch was nearby, and he had the strangest urge to call them and see if he could come visit.

He believed people could change. He'd changed a lot in the course of his forty-five years. But his father hadn't, and Jude hadn't, and as far as Hudson knew, Jan had spent a day near Thanksgiving last year with his family. At the invitation of his mother. Six months after their divorce.

Brent had refused to go, and it had turned into quite the family fight. And yet Jan had gone, and Hudson's mother had baked all of her favorite things.

He pushed the thoughts out of his mind, and when Adele said, "Give me a couple of hours, okay? It takes a while to smoke brisket," his attention switched to her.

"Brisket?"

"Oh, that got your attention, huh?" She laughed and Hudson grinned.

"Well, yeah. I mean, brisket."

"He's a meat lover," Scarlett said.

"Most men are," Adele said. "Shoot. Should I not be making brisket? Do you think that will entice Carson?"

"Entice him to do what?" Scarlett asked.

Adele folded her arms and said, "I don't know."

Apparently that was the end of the conversation, and Hudson pulled into Scarlett's driveway a few minutes later. Adele practically ran around the house, and Scarlett called, "See you in a bit," after her as she helped Gramps out of the car.

Hudson went with them across the lawn to help Gramps get up the steps and into his recliner. "We'll come get you for lunch," he said. "Okay?"

"All right."

"You want me to bring Hound over?"

"Yes, please," Gramps said. "He likes it when I rub his chin."

Hudson chuckled. "I'm sure he does." He exchanged a glance with Scarlett, and they left the cabin. "You want to walk with me over to my place to get the dog?"

She glanced up into the sky. The clear, blue sky with the blazing sun in it. "Really? You think now's a good time to take a walk? It's hot."

"Exercise is good for you," he said.

Scarlett stopped walking and said, "I've got work to do." She stormed away, and Hudson stood there in the backyard wondering what he'd done wrong.

"Scarlett," he called, but she didn't even turn back. Didn't wave her hand. Just marched up the steps, went inside, and slammed the door behind her. *Slammed* it.

Hudson glanced around like perhaps there'd be someone there who could translate Female. He got he'd done something wrong, but he didn't know what. Suggesting they walk to his cabin to get his dog?

He looked back and forth between the homestead and

Gramps's cabin and decided the safer route would be to go get Hound and then try to deal with Scarlett. He didn't want to miss out on a smoked brisket lunch, and he suddenly understood how Carson must feel around Adele.

The walk from the homestead to his cabin took about ten minutes, because some of those pastures were bigger than they looked. Sawyer had moved in a week or so ago, and he'd chosen the cabin at the very end of the first road. Carson had chosen the one right next to Hudson, at the top of the U-shaped community.

Scarlett even called it the Community, and it seemed Hudson couldn't do anything without thinking about her.

Carson sat on his front steps, his two black labs beside him, his knife making something out of a piece of wood. "Hey," he called as Hudson approached. "Back from church?"

"Yep." Hudson detoured up the sidewalk toward Carson. "Adele says she needs a couple of hours before lunch will be ready."

Carson frowned at his whittling, but there was no evidence of annoyance when he glanced up at Hudson. "Great."

"What's with you two?"

"Oh, she doesn't like me because I have a little bit of money." Carson shook his head, a smile on his face. "I'm not sure why that matters, but apparently, to her, it does." He went back to carving.

"I'm going to get Hound," Hudson said. "Gramps wants him."

"You want to take Tony and Ted?" The dogs lifted their heads when Carson said their names.

"If you want to donate them for the afternoon. Gramps sure does love dogs."

"And you want Gramps to be happy so you can spend time with Scarlett." Carson gave him a knowing smile.

Hudson shrugged, thinking about that missed moment on Friday. "She...." He looked at Carson. "How well do you know women?"

"Well enough to know I don't know anything," he said with a chuckle. "What happened?"

"She's mad at me about something, but all I said was we could walk over here to get Hound. She said it was too hot, and I said exercise was good."

Carson stopped carving and cocked his head. He gave Hudson the courtesy of thinking about it for a few seconds before he said, "I have no idea, man. That sounds innocent enough."

"She got mad and stormed off."

"Well, just go ask her."

Hudson half scoffed and half laughed. "Yeah, you definitely don't know as much about women as you think you do."

Carson laughed outright. "You're so right. If I did, I could figure out how to get Adele to go out with me."

"Maybe use some of that money you've got," Hudson

suggested, backing up a few steps. "See you at lunch." He went next door and found Hound lying on the couch. He got down and came over to Hudson to welcome him home, and he said, "Let's go see Gramps, okay, bud?"

Back outside, he let the dog take care of his business and romp around with Tony and Ted for a minute. "Come on, guys," he said, wondering if twenty minutes stood between him and confronting Scarlett about what he'd said.

He walked back over to Gramps's cabin, saying, "We're back," as he opened the door and let the dogs in. "Carson sent over Tony and Ted too."

Gramps grinned at the dogs. "Oh, good."

Hudson let the dogs go over to him, tails wagging, noses sniffing, as he walked into the kitchen to get water for the animals. He filled three bowls and set them by the back door. Only Hound came over to drink, and Hudson sat on the couch beside Gramps's recliner.

"You okay?" he asked the older man.

"Yeah," Gramps said. "My hip is bothering me. Those hard benches really do a number on it."

"Need some pills?" Hudson hoped he'd say no. Gramps had a dozen pill bottles lining the counter in the kitchen.

"Oh, I'm fine. I'm just old. It'll be okay."

"Have you ever had brisket?" Hudson asked, prolonging the moment until he'd have to decide if he'd go talk to Scarlett or go home and take a nap instead.

"A few times," Gramps said. "Adele's always cooking something next door. She brings me things sometimes, late at night."

"She does?" Hudson asked. "How late at night?"

"Oh, nine or ten. Right about the time I wake up from my evening nap. I eat, get up my energy, and I can get down the hall to bed." He grinned, the life and sparkle in his eyes as bright as Hudson had ever seen it. As far as he knew, he'd only called Scarlett the wrong name that one time. His scans and tests had all come back negative, though the doctor had said he had the early stages of dementia.

Scarlett had been upset for a couple of days, and then she hadn't brought it up again. Hudson exhaled as he stood up. "Well, I have to go talk to Scarlett." He'd made it to the front door before turning back to Gramps. "Do you know why she might be upset that I suggested a walk?"

"Now?" Gramps asked. "It's a million degrees."

"Yeah, she said that." Hudson couldn't figure it out, and he decided he better just go straight to the source. So he left Gramps's cabin, crossed the lawn, and rapped lightly on the back door.

Scarlett didn't come, and he knocked louder the second time. It felt like an extraordinary amount of time passed, and he lifted his fist to pound this time. The door got whipped open and Scarlett stood there, her pretty, flowery dress gone. Now she wore a pair of dark gray leggings with a teal T-shirt, and her hair, which had been straight and shiny for church, was twisted on top of her head and secured in a knot.

"What?" she asked.

Hudson flinched at the harshness in her voice. He wanted to throw her attitude right back at her, but decided to take a softer approach. "What did I do wrong?"

"When?"

"Come on, Scarlett." He was much too old for games and decided to tell her that.

Her eyebrows went up so high, they almost touched her hairline. "You don't want to play games?"

"Not particularly," he said. "So I said or did something that upset you, and I just need you to tell me what it was."

"You called me fat," she said.

"What?" Hudson felt like someone had filled his body cavity with ice water. "I did not."

"You said exercise is good for you, as if I *needed* the exercise."

He held up both hands in a universal *I-mean-no-harm* gesture. "I absolutely did not. I was simply saying I wanted you to come over to my cabin with me, hold my hand, and maybe I'd kiss you over there since we got interrupted over here." Hudson's eyes widened and he stepped back, his confession racing from one ear to the next. Had he really just said all that?

The back porch wasn't that big, and he almost fell off. He stumbled and threw his hand out to grab onto the doorframe, adrenaline mixing with pure humiliation.

"Whoa," Scarlett said, grabbing onto his arm too. He steadied himself and looked at her again.

He drew in a breath and decided to keep talking. "I do not think you're fat."

"I'm not skinny."

"I don't like skinny."

She rolled her eyes. "If you say there's more of me to love, you're fired."

Hudson said, "I wasn't going to say that," though the thought had just run through his mind.

"Good idea," Scarlett said dryly.

Hudson swallowed, his blood on fire, which was surely affecting his thought processes. Because he said, "I think you're absolutely gorgeous."

Her expression softened, and she leaned into the doorframe now. "Is that so?"

"It absolutely is so," he said. "And I don't care if you walk or don't walk. I just wanted to spend some time with you this afternoon." He looked over her shoulder but could only see the utility room. "Are you really working?"

"No," she said. "It's nice to have a day off, you know?"

"Oh, I know." He took off his cowboy hat and ran his hand through his hair before repositioning the hat. "I have so much to do this week, but I'm not starting until tomorrow morning."

"You better come in so I'm not air conditioning the whole ranch." Scarlett stepped back to give him room to enter, and he squeezed past her. Hudson's pulse rippled like a flag in a stiff breeze, because he was alone with Scarlett again.

She stepped into the kitchen and pulled out a soda. "You want something to drink?"

"Just water," he said, joining her. "And I can get it." They performed a dance in the kitchen as she got down a glass and passed it to him. He filled it with ice from the freezer while she popped the top on her soda, and then he moved behind her to get to the sink.

He drank half the glass, relief spreading through him with the cool liquid. "I really am sorry."

"It's okay," she said. "I'm a little sensitive about my weight, I guess."

Hudson swept one arm around her waist, his desire for her doubling and then tripling. "I don't know why. You're beautiful."

"Thank you," she murmured.

"I'm very attracted to you," he said, and wow, he needed a mute button. And someone not driven by an insane desire to kiss this woman to push the button so he'd stop saying everything he thought.

Scarlett smiled and tipped up onto her toes. But her kiss missed his mouth, landing instead on his cheek.

"Oh, you're not nice," he whispered, a chuckle coming with the words. "I see how it is."

"I don't think you do," she whispered.

He wrapped his other arm around her and swayed. "Then tell me."

"I'm...a little nervous. I haven't kissed anyone in a long, long time."

"You didn't date after you and Vance broke up?"

"I wasn't going to date while I was still married," she said. "And the divorce was just barely final a few months ago."

Hudson admired her commitment, even to something that was broken. "I haven't had a first date or a first kiss in thirteen years," he said, making today officially Honesty Day.

"So maybe you'll be bad at it too."

"Scarlett, you're not going to be bad at it."

"You don't know that."

Oh, but he did. So he said, "Yes, I do," and tipped his head down, one hand coming up to swipe his cowboy hat right off his head so it wouldn't be in the way.

Shouting met his ears, and he cocked his head to hear better.

"That's Adele," Scarlett said and she obviously heard her best friend say, "Get off my porch!" because Adele was screaming the words.

"I'm going to kill her," Scarlett said, wiggling out of his embrace and heading for the back door. Hudson sighed, put his hat back on, and followed her. They stood on the back porch and watched as Carson moved down the steps, his face one of anger too.

"I wasn't coming in," he said loudly. "Jeez. I *knocked*. I didn't see anything. What are you doing in there anyway?"

He shook his head as he marched away. "You know what? It doesn't matter. I don't care. You're crazy."

"You're uninvited to lunch," Adele called after him, her face one of pure fury.

Hudson put his hand in Scarlett's and squeezed. "You better go talk to her."

"Yeah, she's crying." Scarlett looked up at him and said, "I'm sorry."

"It's fine. Go."

"She never cries."

"Better go then, before she closes that door. It seems hard to get through it." He glanced at the corner of the house as Carson disappeared around it. Scarlett slipped away from him, crossed the lawn quickly, and put her arm around Adele. They did go into the cabin together, leaving Hudson to wonder if he'd ever get his first kiss with the gorgeous, curvy Scarlett Adams.

Chapter Eleven

Scarlett cast a look over her shoulder when she reached Adele's front door. Hudson still stood on her back porch, and the flame inside Scarlett's chest burned like an inferno.

"He is impossible," Adele said, practically a shout. "Impossible!" The yell made Scarlett flinch away from her.

Then she put her arm around Adele, who was crying—a real rarity for the Southern belle who'd been through a lot to get where she was. Of course, Adele had lost everything when Hank had walked out on her, except her debts, all the calls from the credit card companies, and her dignity.

"Okay," Scarlett said. "Come on. Let's get inside." She guided Adele into her cabin, the scent of browned meat and sweet cream making her mouth water. As soon as the door closed, Scarlett added, "I'm seriously annoyed with you, but I love you. So what in the world is going on?"

Adele sniffed and wiped her face. "You're annoyed with me? Because I yelled at some stupid cowboy?"

Scarlett sighed and ran her hands down her face. "No, sweetie. I don't care if you like Carson or not, but you do need to figure out how to get along with him." She looked at her friend. "This is the second time you've interrupted me and Hudson. I swear, if he doesn't kiss me soon...." She shook her head and looked again.

"You were going to kiss him?"

"Yes, just now." Scarlett smiled but couldn't meet her friend's eyes. "It's fine. Nothing."

"I'm so sorry, Scarlett." Adele sounded apologetic, and Scarlett waved her words away.

"It's fine. It'll happen when it's supposed to happen." If only her every cell didn't crave his kiss. She looked around the cabin, her attention going easily to the bright lights in the kitchen.

Abnormally bright. These were stage lights, all shining down on the countertop, which was a deep, black granite. That hadn't been in the cabin when they'd come to the ranch several weeks ago.

Nor had the pan rack hanging over the island, or the video camera attached to the rack.

"What is going on here?" she asked, taking a step toward the kitchen at the back of the house. "You're doing videos?" Adele had always wanted to be a chef, but Scarlett thought that dream had died years ago, when she'd met and married Hank.

"It's nothing," Adele said, darting in front of her. But the equipment couldn't be concealed, even by Adele's size-fourteen body.

"This is not nothing," Scarlett said, running her fingers along the cool granite. "Where did this come from?"

"A friend of Hank's owed me a favor," she said. "He brought it a few weeks ago."

"The mysterious delivery you got."

"I'm not doing anything illegal." Adele picked up a wooden spoon and stirred whatever was in that big pot. It smelled like cream and something sweet. "This is still okay."

"Still okay," Scarlett echoed, peering up at the lights and seeing four cameras. This was a serious set-up, with some serious monetary investment here. "Adele, what are you doing?"

"I make those food videos you love," she said, adding a bowl of white liquid to the pot. She stirred it around like a professional, though she'd never attended culinary school.

Scarlett watched as she added a pinch of salt and pepper that she'd already pre-measured, then a chunk of butter. "What are you making?" She wanted to ask a lot of questions, but she didn't want Adele to start screaming at her. She'd been friends with her for a long time, and if she handled her with kid gloves, Adele would start talking soon enough.

There was no music. Adele didn't say anything. She just stirred everything together, flipped off the single burner, and stepped back from the counter.

"I'm TastySpot." She pulled out her phone, swiped, tapped, and handed the device to Scarlett.

Scarlett took the phone but didn't look at it. "Tasty-Spot? Are you kidding me?" She glanced at the phone, at a video of coconut curry chicken chowder—which she'd watched a couple of weeks ago.

"I've seen all of your videos." A sense of numbness spread through Scarlett. It was like she couldn't get her thoughts to move, as if they'd been encased in molasses.

"Yes, well, my account is just now getting big enough to make a few dollars."

Scarlett looked at the video again, swiping to the next one. "I wanted to make your cinnamon pull-apart bread. It looked so good."

"It was good," Adele said. "Gramps keeps asking for it."

Scarlett jerked her head back up and found Adele wearing a sly smile. "You're giving all the food to Gramps?" Annoyance surged through her again. "Are you *freaking* kidding me? I'm giving you somewhere free to live. Paying you to train goats to jump on people's backs. And you're giving all this deliciousness to *Gramps*?"

Adele had the decency to look slightly ashamed. "My freezer is packed." She stepped over to the chest freezer Scarlett hadn't seen, glancing in the pot as she went and finding creamed corn. That would go well with the brisket.

"I figured I'd tell you eventually," Adele said. "And you'd be mad, and I'd hoped you'd be pacified by this." She opened the freezer and stepped back.

Scarlett felt like lightning had struck her now, and everything was moving too fast. The cabin was boiling hot from all the lights shining down on that black surface. She hurried over to the freezer to find zipper bags and plastic containers, all neatly stacked and labeled. "Oh, my gosh! You have the chicken chowder right there."

"Take it."

Scarlett looked at her friend, eyes wide. "Really?"

"There's some of the gazpacho in there too."

"I so hate you right now," Scarlett said, reaching into the freezer. She pulled out several containers. "You're feeding me and Hudson until I get my kiss."

Adele started laughing, and Scarlett couldn't help joining her. She put all the food she wanted on the counter and turned to hug Adele. "I'm sorry about Carson. Do you want me to fire him?"

"No, but...kind of."

"Good, because I can't afford to lose him. He's a career cowboy, and I have a meeting with him later about how to run a ranch, the employees I need, how to manage the money and the herd." The sheer amount of what she didn't know seemed to press her into the ground.

"Career cowboy, right." Adele scoffed and stepped out

of Scarlett's embrace. "Have you seen his jeans? He must have a hundred pairs, because they're never dirty. It's like he's never ridden a horse before."

Scarlett blinked, reeling the same way she had when she'd first seen all the camera equipment. "Oh my—you *like* him."

"I do not." Adele rolled her eyes and stepped over to the hotplate to check the creamed corn. She stirred it and replaced the lid.

"You do too," Scarlett said, deciding to push this. "*I* haven't noticed his jeans. *I'm* not looking at his clothes. You are. You *like* him."

"He's arrogant," Adele said. "So full of himself. And he clearly has a lot of money."

"Maybe not as much as you think," Scarlett said. "I mean, if he's got a hundred pairs of jeans."

"Oh, jeez," Adele said in a dry tone. "He sold his ranch in Montana for billions. I looked it up online."

Scarlett's laughter filled the cabin as she picked up the food she'd taken from the freezer. She headed for the front door, half-hopeful that Hudson would still be standing on her back porch.

"What?" Adele called after her, but Scarlett just shook her head, still laughing.

"Get over your phobia of rich men," Scarlett said. "And maybe give Carson a chance."

"Right." Adele glared from the kitchen as Scarlett

opened the front door. "And lock that behind you. I don't want him trying to barge in here again."

"Maybe he's just hungry." Scarlett juggled the containers and bags, trying to get a couple of fingers around the doorknob. "Can you look *that* up online?" She finally got her thumb on one side and her ring finger on the other and managed to move the doorknob enough to get the latch to release.

"I don't like him just because I looked him up online," Adele said.

"Of course not," Scarlett said. "I regularly Google people I don't care about, just for fun." She gave Adele a knowing look and ducked out of the cabin before Adele could find something to throw at her, a giggle still tickling the back of her throat.

Scarlett was not laughing after her meeting with Carson the following morning. She had six pages of notes, and no idea how to accomplish any of the things he'd suggested. He'd left through the front door to get over to the Goat Grounds, and Scarlett hadn't had the heart to ask him how things were going over there.

He hadn't said anything about Adele, which spoke to his character. He seemed the same as when he'd arrived, and Scarlett had taken a peek at his jeans when he'd left.

So they were clean. Didn't mean he didn't know what he was talking about.

Because he obviously did. He'd suggested she hire an accountant for a place like this, especially if they were going to be getting funding from non-profit organizations like Forever Friends.

He'd suggested they have a foreman over every area of the ranch—the dogs, the cats, the goats, all of them. That was six people, plus someone over the agriculture and land development. He said she had a lot of land here, and it wasn't being used to its full potential.

"I like it wild," she'd said, and he'd said it didn't have to be cultivated or have a building on it to be used better.

She liked Carson, no matter what Adele said, and she was glad he'd come to Last Chance Ranch. So she'd put up another ad for more help. Now that Hudson was selling cars, she had a little bit of money for things.

And if she could get Forever Friends to approve her ranch for an animal sanctuary....

She didn't want to get her hopes up too high. She'd been in situations before where they crashed, and it always took a few months for her to get back to herself. But she didn't want to be hopeless or fatalistic either.

Realistic, she told herself. That was what she needed to be. And she could work hard and get as much done as possible before Jewel and her crew came to the ranch to assess it.

She stood up and left the house through the front door

too, leaving her notes on the kitchen table. Hudson said he'd be working on the signs that morning, and she wanted to see his progress. Then she needed to work in the buildings she'd gone through with him last week. Hang some art on the walls. Put up a couple of tables and a desk that should be delivered this afternoon. And Adele had invited her to a practice goat yoga session that evening.

If she could get the last two cars off the lawn, and the signs up, and the robot mailbox fixed, this ranch might start to feel like home. Oh, and she needed to finish the buildings before Jewel went through them, and put up more help wanted ads, and make sure someone went out to feed the llamas....

One thing at a time, she coached herself, taking a moment to enjoy the fresh air out here. She'd never breathed air like this in the city, and she paused to listen to the silence in the country. She'd always loved city life, but there was something alluring about the country too.

She felt freer out here than she ever had in LA. No traffic. No smog. No hustle and bustle, or worry about what her boss would say about her proposals and mockups. The pressures were different, sure, and in that moment, Scarlett realized she'd rather stress over signs and feeding schedules for pigs than Fortune 500 marketing campaigns.

And she didn't quite know what to do with that feeling, but it made her smile. So did the sound of hammering as she got closer to Hudson's cabin. And the sight of

Hound as he trotted down the lane to meet her, as if he knew she'd be coming at precisely this time.

"Thank you, Lord," she whispered to the clear sky, so grateful that she was where she was supposed to be, even if she'd never envisioned herself on this ranch. After all, life rarely turned out exactly how she'd planned—but it was always good.

Chapter Twelve

Hudson nailed the boards he'd carved together in order, sweat already pouring down his face though it was only mid-morning. His stomach growled, but he kept the hammer moving, determined to get all the signs done before lunch.

Hound got up from the porch and started down the steps, panting as he went. But Carson wasn't home, and his two dogs were inside the air-conditioned cabin. Someone was coming. Hudson didn't bother to call after his golden retriever, and he placed the top board on the sign for the Goat Grounds. This sign would need to be set first, because the goat yoga was starting on Saturday.

His phone flashed with a blue light, which meant he had texts. He ignored them as he caught sight of Scarlett rounding the corner and walking toward him. The sight of her almost had him hitting his thumb with the hammer, and he focused on finishing this sign before she completed the half-block walk to him.

Could he gather her into his arms and kiss her when she arrived? He couldn't stop thinking about kissing her, especially now that she'd basically given her permission for him to do so.

"Hey," she called when she reached the grass where he'd set up a make-shift wood shop.

"Morning," he said, driving in one more nail and then lifting the sign. "What do you think?"

Her eyes traced the letters and then roamed back to his. "It's great, Hudson."

"I just need to paint it and then seal the wood." He looked at the sign, which read GOAT GROUNDS in huge, raised letters, one word on top of the others. "I've done all the carving. Well, Carson did a majority of it. He's so much faster than I am."

It had been a decently pleasant few hours while they'd worked together on his porch yesterday afternoon. He'd said nothing about the argument with Adele, and Hudson didn't know him well enough to bring it up either. They'd both missed the lunch, because Scarlett had texted him to say Adele wasn't going to make brisket.

So while Hudson had wanted a day of rest, he'd carved the signs while talking to another cowboy. All in all, it wasn't the worst way to spend a Sunday afternoon, but it certainly wasn't the kissing he wanted to do with Scarlett.

"I can help paint for a while," she said. "Then I'm

going to get the volunteer center set up once the furniture comes."

"Great," Hudson said. "Let's get the paint out." He moved out from behind the workbench and headed for the gravel that lined the front of the house. He'd stashed the paint cans there, as well as all the brushes and trays for the different colors.

"So what color do you want?" he asked, bending to pick up the drop cloth. She could paint in the shade on the side of the cabin, or on the porch. "And where do you want to be?"

"I don't know," she said.

"I'll put this on the porch," he said. "It's decently shady, at least until lunchtime." He stepped around her as she crouched down to examine the paint cans.

He spread the cloth out to protect the porch as Hound came gingerly back up the steps. "Hey, buddy," he said, giving the dog an affectionate pat. He lay right in the middle of the cloth, as if Hudson had put it there just for him. He chuckled and said, "Go on, bud. You're not going to be able to stay there."

Hound blinked at him, and Hudson went back down the steps. "Hound's in your way."

Scarlett looked up at him, her beautiful eyes a bit unfocused. She blinked and said, "I'll get him to move," before going back to the paint cans.

Hudson returned to his workbench and started piecing together the sign for LlamaLand. He started nailing it together, only looking up when Scarlett asked, "What about rainbow?" She straightened and brushed her hands along her thighs as she came back toward him. "I could do a different color for each letter, in a pattern."

"Sure," he said. "Whatever you want. It's your ranch." He grinned at her.

"Any word on the other cars?" she asked.

"I've got a ton of texts," he said, fitting another nail into place. "I was hoping they'd all be from you." He gave her what he hoped was a flirty look and went right back to his work, his internal temperature a little hotter simply because she was near him.

"Oh, you were, were you?"

"Well, yeah," he said. "Maybe asking me to lunch."

"I asked you to lunch last night," she said. "You forgot?"

"I didn't forget."

"Can I look at your phone?"

"Sure." He nodded to where it sat on the corner of the workbench. "I can run down and meet someone whenever. That is, if my lunch date is flexible." He caught her smile out of the corner of his eye, and then she focused on his phone.

He'd hammered in one nail when she said, "Hudson, I think you better get down to the cars."

"Why?" He set the hammer down. "Something wrong?"

She lifted her gaze from the phone. "No, something's

right. This guy says he's looking at the car and wants to buy it." She handed the device back to him, and Hudson read the texts quickly.

"All right. I'll head down."

"Can I come?"

"Sure." He jogged over to the front steps and went up them to get inside the house. He grabbed his keys from the kitchen counter and headed back outside. Scarlett was already in the truck, and he joined her.

"I have a guy coming to look at the truck tonight," he said.

"I saw the texts." She twirled a piece of hair between her fingers and watched him.

"What?" he asked, glad his cabin was only five minutes up the road from where he'd parked the cars.

"You're just cute."

"Cute?" he repeated. "Oh, no man my age wants to be called cute."

"No?" She laughed. "What would be better? Handsome?"

"Definitely."

"Hot?"

"Uh, I guess," he said. "But that's more of a teenage thing, and sweetheart, I'm a long way from a teenager."

"You and me both."

He glanced at her, some of the playfulness definitely gone from her voice in that last statement. "Is it still rude to ask a woman her age?"

"I'm forty-three," she said.

"Oh, so I win." He flashed her a smile as he went past the still-legless robot mailbox. "Forty-five."

"Married for how long?" she asked, a measure of challenge in her tone now.

"Ten years," he said, his fingers tightening around the wheel at this topic.

"Dang, you win again," she said. "Only six for me."

"No kids?"

"No," she said too quickly.

Hudson let a few seconds of silence go by, but he didn't want to let her hide from him. He wanted to know everything about her. "I sense a story there."

"We had...some trouble getting pregnant," she said. "It drove us apart instead of together."

"I'm sorry," he said.

"We got two dogs," she said. "Billy and Bob. They were—are—English retrievers."

"No wonder Hound likes you so much."

"I lost them to my ex," she said, her voice almost a ghost of itself. "He won them in the settlement."

Hudson remembered her saying that now. He didn't know how to comfort her, and he liked the playful, flirty version of Scarlett more than this one. But he knew there were dozens of sides to a person, and he wanted to see all of hers.

He didn't apologize again. He simply reached over and took her hand in his, squeezing tightly for a moment before the car and the truck came into view. "He's still here. Good." He released her hand, but she kept a grip on his.

"You didn't tell me if you had kids."

The pain in his chest came instantly, and it ripped through him hotly. "No," he said. "No kids. Jan, uh, didn't want them."

"Did you?"

Hudson flicked his gaze to the man waiting beside the blue car Hudson would like to sell and back to Scarlett. "Yes," he said honestly, swallowing a moment later. "Jan didn't want to lose her figure."

Saying it out loud sounded stupid, but he'd loved and respected Jan. He'd gone along with what she'd wanted, because his sole goal was to make her happy. Foolishness raced through him, and he ducked his head and got out of the truck, glad Scarlett let go of his hand and let him go.

"Hey," he said to the man standing there. "Sorry, I didn't see your texts right away."

"It's okay," he said. "I'm Jake."

"Hudson." They shook hands. "You're interested in the car?"

"Yeah, my son needs something to get to football practice."

"I've got the keys right here," he said as a tall, gangly boy got out of the other car parked there. "You can take it for a spin." He handed the keys to the father, who passed them to his son. The boy pushed his long hair out of his face and gave Hudson a tentative smile.

"Be back in a few minutes," the father said before folding himself into the car, and Hudson watched as they pulled up the stop sign and turned left.

Scarlett joined him, her hands tucked into her back pockets. "I'm sorry about your wife."

"Ex-wife," he said automatically. "And it's fine. Old water, under an old bridge." Thankfully, she didn't say anything else, and Hudson sold the blue car to the teenager and his father when they returned from their test drive.

He flipped through the cash as he and Scarlett got back in the truck, and she laughed. "Give me my cut, cowboy."

"Oh, I'm a cowboy now?"

"You've been a cowboy since I met you." She nodded at his hat. "You never take that thing off."

"Sure I do," he said.

"When?" she challenged.

"Well, if you'll recall, I took it off yesterday in your house, right before I wanted to kiss you." He looked at her, no one else on the road going back up to the ranch.

"Mm," she said, her eyes absolutely glittering at him. "I'd like to see that happen again."

"I bet you would." He chuckled as he went past the robot and down his street, his own blood burning for the chance to kiss her.

"Maybe at lunch today," she said, and Hudson's hopes soared sky-high.

"Maybe," he said, teasing her and enjoying it so, so much. Now, he just had to make it to lunch without nailing one of his fingers to the signs because he couldn't concentrate with her so dang close, and maybe he'd get his kiss today after all.

Maybe you should lock Adele in her house as a precaution....

Chapter Thirteen

Scarlett enjoyed the up and down movement of painting, the way the letters came to life under the stroke of her brush, the way her mind was able to roam free. She hadn't planned on painting letters that morning, and her to-do list sat there, dormant. But she didn't care.

Hudson whistled while he worked, and she wanted to be close to him. The peace that drifted through her couldn't be found while she obsessed over when the furniture arrived and what she should say when Jewel arrived a week from now.

A week from now. There was so much time between now and then that Scarlett needed to focus on what was right in front of her, not what lay seven days down the road.

So she painted the Goat Grounds sign with blue paint, deciding the rainbow-colored letters were too childish.

Then she did LlamaLand with red and Canine Club in orange. Hudson was much quicker than her, and he joined her about an hour before lunchtime, and he made Feline Frenzy yellow and Horse Heaven green. They worked together on Piggy Paradise in pink, and the flirting between them was shameless.

With the last letter painted, he said, "All right. I'm starving."

She was too, and she stretched her back as he gathered up the painting supplies and cleaned them up. She went down the steps, enjoying the California sunshine, and saw Carson round the corner and continue toward his house, his head down.

"Hey, Carson," she said, causing him to glance up. "Thanks for all the advice you gave me this morning."

A smile burst onto his face, and if Adele thought he wasn't handsome, she was delusional. He even had an adorable dimple in his right cheek, and that cowboy hat made him even more her type.

"Of course," he said. "You guys finish the signs?"

"Yeah, all assembled and painted. Hudson will seal them once the paint dries." She smiled at him, almost inviting him to come to lunch at the homestead. But if he came to lunch at the homestead, she and Hudson wouldn't be alone. And if they weren't alone.... She pressed her lips together. "How's it going in the Goat Grounds?"

"Great," he said with a smile. "I think I know all their names now."

"What did Adele settle on?" she asked. "Candy bars?"

"Ice cream flavors." Carson shook his head, but he didn't look annoyed or dismissive. He looked...appreciative. "And I got all the animals on the south side fed."

"Thanks, Carson. You're a lifesaver."

"Anyway, I've got to let my dogs out." He tipped his hat at her and walked away. He opened the door, and both of his labs burst out of the door, sprinted down the steps, and frolicked with Hound, who managed to get out of the shade in order to greet his doggy friends.

Scarlett laughed and watched the dogs while she waited for Hudson. He finally came out of his place, easily slipping his hand into hers and tugging her toward the road. "So, what's on the menu for today?"

"Okay, so I have a secret," Scarlett said, shooting a glance toward Carson's front door, which was still open. But he wasn't there.

Hudson whistled at Hound, and he came running up beside them, leaving the other two dogs behind. "A secret?"

"Yeah. Have you ever smelled anything around Adele's house?"

"All the time," he said. "She's obviously got time to bake and cook."

"And we saw her yelling at Carson yesterday."

"Right. I spent most of the afternoon and evening with him yesterday, and he didn't say anything."

"Well, I got inside her cabin," Scarlett said, practically

singsonging the words. "And she *is* baking and cooking in there. A lot. Every day. And she's got a freezer full of food. I got some chicken curry chowder, some watermelon gazpacho, and several other things."

"Huh," Hudson said, surprise in his voice. "What's she cooking all that for?"

"That's the secret. How familiar with social media are you?"

"Social media? I used to have one of my guys post for me. Facebook, Instagram, Twitter. But I don't use them myself."

The secret wasn't as juicy if he hadn't seen the videos. She pulled out her phone anyway. "Okay, so these short video clips of recipes are super popular right now. They take you from the beginning of a recipe to the end, all in sixty seconds or less." She navigated to TastySpot and showed him the chicken curry chowder.

He watched it and said, "Wow. I actually like that." He scrolled down and started watching another one, his cowboy boots scuffing the ground.

"Addictive, right?" she asked, attracted to him more because he liked the videos, if that was even possible.

"This fried ice cream looks amazing." He glanced at her. "Do you have any of that?"

"I didn't see any of those," she said. "But the point is, Hudson, TastySpot is run by Adele. *Every* one of those videos she made. *She* made the food *and* the videos."

He looked back at the phone. "There's like a hundred videos here."

"One hundred and twelve," Scarlett said. "I watched a bunch of them last night." She danced a few steps in front of him. "And we get to eat the food."

"All of it?" He handed her the phone back.

"Well, I have a few containers," she said. "And you can't tell anyone. Adele swore me to secrecy." She stopped dead in the middle of the road. "Oh, my gosh. No." She moaned and rolled her shoulders.

"What?" Hudson asked, moving to stand right in front of her.

Scarlett didn't want to say. Her insides squirmed, and she couldn't quite look at Hudson.

"What?" he repeated.

"I told Adele she had to feed me and you until we kissed, because she kept interrupting us." Scarlett muttered the last few words, and she ducked her head so she wouldn't accidentally look at Hudson.

He started laughing, took her hand, and continued walking. "I don't care about food, Scarlett."

"I've never heard a man say that," she said.

"Compared to kissing you?" he asked. "Nothing Adele's made is going to be better than kissing you."

Scarlett paused again. "You think so? You haven't even done it yet."

Hudson turned toward her, his eyes lit up. He took a step back toward her, and it ignited that flame inside her stomach. "I just know." His hand slid along her hip around to her back, bringing her close to him.

"Are you going to take the hat off now?" she whispered, his fingers tiptoeing along her arm to her shoulder before tucking her loose hair behind her ear.

"Do you want me to take off the hat?"

Nerves gathered into a ball of fear in the back of her throat. She hadn't kissed a man in such a long time, but she wanted this cowboy mechanic's lips on hers as soon as possible. "Yes," she whispered.

He moved so slowly, it was agonizing. Her heart pounded and she licked her lips so he wouldn't be kissing her dry mouth. Finally, that hand removed his hat, taking the shade of the brim with it, and he leaned down, his lips barely brushing hers.

The kiss lasted only a moment, and then he growled low in his throat, brought her flush against him, and kissed her.

And she kissed him back, matching him stroke for stroke and enjoying the flapping of wings as they moved through her whole body. Oh, this man could make a woman feel like a treasure. He deepened the kiss, and Scarlett hoped Carson wouldn't come walking down the road.

Hudson finally pulled away, his breath laboring in and out of his mouth. "Wow, Scarlett," he whispered, sweeping his mouth along her jaw to her neck.

"Wow," she repeated, holding onto his wide shoulders

as he touched his lips to her earlobe and then pulled away completely.

"Does this mean we don't get that curry chowder?" he asked, leaning his forehead against hers. "Because if it does, I don't even care. That was worth it."

Scarlett smiled, her eyes still closed. "Maybe what Adele doesn't know won't hurt her."

"She can't eat everything she makes."

"So we don't tell her." She opened her eyes and looked up at him.

"You were going to tell her?"

Scarlett shrugged, a tingling still on her lips. "I mean, we've been best friends since college. So yeah, I'd probably have told her when you *finally* kissed me."

"Hey, *she's* the one who's been interrupting us."

"And she's very sorry," Scarlett said, starting to walk again, her steps much slower now. "That's why we have the food." She linked her hand through Hudson's arm, and put her other hand on his forearm too. They strolled down the dirt road, and the wide open sky held such happiness for Scarlett.

She hadn't felt this level of happiness in such a long time, and she wanted to hold onto it for as long as she could. And it seemed like Hudson did too, which was the strangest thing of all.

A WEEK LATER, Scarlett sat on the front steps of the homestead as the sun rose, trying to think of what she'd overlooked. Carson had installed all of the signs. The buildings were clean and furnished as much as they could be. The animals seemed healthy, and the hay barn was fuller than it had been in a long time.

Later, when Jewel was scheduled to arrive, Gramps would be busy with Hound, Tony, and Ted. Adele's goat yoga had been nothing short of amazing, and the session for that morning would begin in a couple of hours.

Scarlett lifted her coffee mug to her lips and sipped, mentally ticking off each item, like she'd been doing for hours. She once again concluded that she'd done everything she could. "The rest is up to you, Lord," she said to the brightening sky.

Her phone chimed, and she glanced at it on the porch beside her. Hudson's name flashed there, as did the first few words of his message. She couldn't read it fast enough before the screen darkened again, and she took a few seconds to simply think about him as the sun breathed new life into this day.

He made butterflies appear in her stomach with a simple text. A thought about him. A memory of how he cradled her face in both hands while he kissed her. How he held her close to him while the sun dipped low in the sky and they talked about the horses, or the goat yoga class they'd both gone to, or one of Adele's recipes.

Scarlett hadn't been so comfortable with a man in

many years, and she marveled that Hudson made her feel so safe and so cherished through such simple actions.

She set down her mug and picked up her phone. Hudson's text read, *Down at the mailbox. Prime will be done in time, I promise.*

He'd messaged again while she'd been thinking about him, and his second message said, *Want to come keep me company?*

Of course she did, and Scarlett left her coffee cup on the porch and headed for her car. After the quick drive down the road, she found Hudson kneeling in front of the robot mailbox, a welding mask over his face.

Sparks flew, and he continued working while she parked next to his truck, which had the tailgate open and all his tools lying there.

"Hey," she said once he stopped working.

"Morning," he said, standing, flipping his mask back, and coming toward her. He leaned down and kissed her, even his fast hello kisses sensual and complete. "How does he look?" He stepped out of the way so she could see the beloved robot from her childhood.

Prime had gotten two new legs, both with twisty pieces that added fresh character to his personality. The bottom of the mailbox had been replaced, which meant Last Chance Ranch could now get mail without it being left on the ground. And the glass in the chest cavity had been replaced and gleamed in the brightening sun.

"He looks so great." She wrapped both arms around Hudson. "Thank you so much for working on this."

"Is the car down at the bottom of the road okay?" he asked. "Or should I move it up to the parking lot?"

"I think it's okay there," she said. "You really are a miracle worker." She beamed up at him, wondering what she'd done to get a man like him in her life. On her ranch. Had God really let Scooby out to bring Hudson in her life? Did He care about small details like that?

Pastor Williams would say that yes, He did. That God concerned Himself with the details of our lives, all the small details. Scarlett wanted to ask why during that sermon, but the preacher had answered that too.

Because He loves you.

"I fixed a few cars," Hudson said.

"And made a bunch of signs, and sold the cars, and fixed my robot."

"Well, the robot's not done yet. He still needs a fresh coat of paint." He glanced at his watch. "And I have just enough time to get it done, if you'll stop distracting me."

"I'm not distracting you. You asked me—" She had to stop talking when he kissed her, and she playfully shoved him away. "Hey, who's distracting who?"

He chuckled and pulled his welding mask off his head. He tossed it in the back of his truck and reached for the painting supplies. Whistling, he swiped the paint onto the metal, and Scarlett had never found a man sexier than she did in that moment, watching Hudson.

The details got added with accent colors of red, yellow, and blue, and Hudson stood back and said, "There. He's done."

"Good, she's going to be here any minute." She helped him pack up the brushes and cans, and he'd just closed the tailgate of his truck when the rumbling of an engine filled the air.

A big engine.

Scarlett turned to face the road to see a brigade of three black SUVs coming toward them. They stopped, their mirrored windows more intimidating than anything else.

"Here we go," Scarlett said, drawing in a deep breath. "You're with me, right?"

Chapter Fourteen

Hudson wished he'd had time to return to his cabin and wash his hands. But Jewel and her team were here, and all he could say to Scarlett was, "Right here with you."

The driver's door of the first SUV opened, and an older woman slid to the ground. She had white hair that fell to her shoulders, and she seemed to wear a perpetual smile the way Hound did. She wore a gray T-shirt that said *Forever Friends* on the front of it in bright orange letters, the O shaped like a paw print.

"You must be Scarlett," she said, moving forward. "I'm Jewel."

Scarlett held very still, and Hudson nudged her. She lunged forward and said, "I am Scarlett. Good to meet you." She extended her hand, but Jewel drew her right into a hug. If Scarlett minded, she didn't say anything.

"This is my partner, Hudson Flannigan." Scarlett cleared her throat, their eyes meeting for just a moment, before she turned back to Jewel.

"Nice to meet you," Hudson said, his mind screaming *partner*? What did that mean? Partner on the ranch? Life partner? Sure, he liked Scarlett. *Really* liked Scarlett. But he also *really* wanted a definition for the word partner. Her definition.

"Oh, look at this pup." Jewel crouched down and gave Hound the rub down of his life. He grinned up at her, his tail thwapping the ground in bliss. "We just got a cute pair of dogs at our shelter in the city." She looked up at Scarlett. "But it's full."

"So what will happen to them?" she asked.

Jewel straightened. "Well, we've already established Los Angeles as a no-kill city, so we'll try to find them a home or we'll send them to another facility."

"What if there isn't another facility?" Scarlett asked.

"Well, we're hoping it'll be yours," Jewel said with a smile. "Should we park here and go in?"

"No," Scarlett said. "No, we have a parking lot at the Goat Grounds, where our goat yoga classes are held. Let's go up there."

Jewel nodded, and Scarlett dug in her pocket for her keys. "You can follow us," she said, and Hudson got the unspoken message that he'd be leaving his truck right where it was. So he got in the passenger seat with Scarlett behind the wheel and all of her nerves between them.

"It's going to be okay," he said.

"I know that," she said, a definite snap to her voice. "I don't need you to tell me that."

Hudson blinked. "Sorry."

She sighed, and Hudson didn't even really dare to look at her. "No, I'm sorry," she said. "I'm just so nervous."

"The ranch is amazing," he said. "We've done everything we can to make it presentable." He'd been on the ranch for almost three weeks, and even he was impressed with how much it had changed.

Everything was neat and trimmed now, even all the weeds along the road leading in. The fences had been fixed, and the animals were healthy.

"Shoot," Scarlett said as she turned into the parking lot. "Maybe having a goat yoga class while Jewel was here was a bad idea. The lot's full."

"There's room on the street," he said, trying to be calm without being condescending. He didn't want to get snapped at again. He pushed aside his hurt feelings. After all, he'd had bad days too. Said things he wished he hadn't. And she'd apologized immediately.

She pulled back onto the road and parked facing the fence, Jewel and her team following her. Everyone got out of the cars, and Hudson shook hands with eleven other people. Eleven. His nerves zipped around in his body, and he didn't really have anything at stake here.

Of course you do, he said, his gaze flickering to Scarlett for a moment. She was absolutely on fire, smiling and nodding and asking questions. He liked her, and this was important to her, and he really wanted the tour to go well.

"So this is our goat facility," Scarlett said. "We do goat yoga here with our baby Norwegian goats, and there's a class in session right now." She stepped over to the area that had been fenced for the class, and it was dirt ground with lots of straw on it. There were thirty people in the class, and Adele up front, leading them in a clear, loud voice.

Carson moved through the exercisers, something in his hands as he moved the goats through the crowd so everyone got an experience with a goat jumping on them while they did their yoga poses.

Hudson smiled at the cute little animals, and Scarlett answered all the questions anyone had before moving them over to the pens where they kept all of the goats. "Adults don't do the yoga," she said, indicating the several out in the pasture. "And they share their facilities with the few cattle we have here on the ranch."

"How many people do you have working in this area?" Jewel asked.

"Just two right now," Scarlett said. "Adele, the instructor, and her partner Carson. I have a third man, Sawyer, who takes care of the cattle." She swallowed, and Hudson had the urge to slip his hand into hers. But he didn't.

They walked along the pens and crossed the street to the Canine Club, the bright orange letters making him smile. In fact, Jewel and her team crowded around the sign and had Scarlett take their picture.

"We have twenty-six dogs here right now," Scarlett said. "My grandfather manages their care, and we have a few volunteers each day to help with meals and walks." She pushed through the gate, and Hudson held it for everyone.

"The enclosures are temperature regulated," he said, bringing up the rear. "But most of the dogs like hanging around outside."

"We let them go in and out as they please," Scarlett said, the perfect tag-team. "Except if they're sick or hurt. We have separate accommodations for them."

Jewel and her team looked through everything, and the man closest to Hudson, whose name was Thomas Disher, said, "This is a great place. I'm surprised it's not a Forever Friends affiliate already."

"It used to be," Jewel said, that smile on her face.

"What?" Scarlett asked, stepping next to Hudson. "It was?"

"A long time ago," she said, nodding to her left. "I remember when we poured the foundation for that building."

Hudson turned to see her looking at the buildings on the other side of Canine Club, that he and Scarlett had cleaned, dusted, painted, and furnished.

"It was my first year working for the organization," she

said. "So when was that?" She exhaled and looked at another woman.

They said, "Twenty-four years," together, Jewel's more of a question than a statement.

"I can't believe that," Scarlett said. "My grandfather didn't say anything."

"Oh, it was your grandmother who worked with us," Jewel said. "Janice, right?"

"Yes," Scarlett said, slipping into that freeze-mode again.

"Let's go see how those buildings have fared," Jewel said. "I think they stopped working with us about a decade ago." She walked beside Scarlett now, tapping the tops of the fence posts as they walked toward the parking lot that separated the cat facility from the administration buildings. "Your grandmother got sick, and it just became too much for her."

"Yes," Scarlett said, though Hudson had the distinct impression she didn't know about her grandmother's illness. "Well, I'm running the ranch now, and I'd love to partner up with you again."

They went through the buildings, the Feline Frenzy facilities, and moved over to the larger animal areas. Hudson spoke about the horses, and Sawyer came out and talked about the pigs and llamas, and they looped back around by the homestead.

"Well, this place is still in great shape," Jewel said. "Natalie, what do you think?"

"I think they can take on at least two dozen more horses and feed them off the land," she said. "And Utah's full right now."

"Jerry?"

"Our cat needs aren't pressing right now, but she's got room here if we need it."

"It's the dog space we need," Thomas said. "And she's got that too."

"With room to grow," Jewel said, turning back to Scarlett. "We'd love to partner with you, with specific needs for dogs and horses. Would you be willing to construct more buildings for more dogs?"

She looked at Hudson, as if he'd be able to give her the go-ahead. He nodded once before she turned back to Jewel and said, "I don't see why not. The ranch you toured today is only about a third of the land at Last Chance Ranch."

"And isn't the name perfect?" Jewel laughed and surveyed her crew. "And I don't know about you, but I love that this is a working ranch, a rescue ranch, and an interactive ranch. Goat yoga? Genius." She shook her head, that grin perfectly in place.

"So I'll get the papers out of the truck," a woman named Adrian said.

"Papers?" Scarlett practically screeched the words, and Hudson stepped over to her and slipped his fingers into hers.

"We're ready to sign if you are," Jewel said, looking at Scarlett now. "I mean, I can see you care about this place, and it's in better shape than when the ranch was partnered with us before."

Hudson had a hard time believing that, but he kept his mouth shut. Adrian returned to the SUV and came back with papers, which Scarlett started signing as Jewel explained when the funding would come, and how, and what reports would need to be turned in, and when.

Hudson tapped out some notes on his phone, because Scarlett was overwhelmed and simply kept nodding and signing, signing and nodding.

When the dust from the tires of the three SUVs finally settled, Hudson felt like he needed a nap.

"Wow," he said. "That was the most intense hour of my life."

"I can't believe they brought papers with them." She turned toward him, her smile spreading across her beautiful face. She leapt into his arms, and Hudson grinned as he caught her around the waist.

"They brought papers with them," she said, laughing now.

"And you were worried," he said, chuckling with her. He set her on her feet and grinned down at her. "You were amazing, by the way. Everything you said sounded professional and true and...just amazing." He leaned down and kissed her, his desire for her reaching epic proportions.

Every kiss felt like the first one, and he kneaded her closer, and then closer still. If he rounded up his age, he'd be fifty, but she made him feel like a sixteen-year-old experiencing his first female touch.

He growled softly in the back of his throat and pressed her into the front door behind her, placing his feet between hers. "Scarlett," he murmured, not sure what else he wanted to say. He didn't want to say anything. He just wanted to kiss her. So he kept doing that.

Chapter Fifteen

Scarlett hummed as she chopped watermelon into cubes. Adele had planned a big Fourth of July celebration for the humans at Last Chance Ranch, and that number had swelled to eight over the course of the last few weeks.

All volunteers had been invited to the picnic too, and Hudson was currently standing in the back yard with David Merrill, who'd been hired to roam from place to place and take care of outbuildings, fences, facilities, and more. If the air conditioning went out in a dog enclosure, David took care of it. If a fence rung got broken, David fixed it. If the pigs got a little too excited in their play and knocked over a trough, David fixed it.

Sawyer was helping them put up a huge tent, and Carson worked with another new addition, Cache Bryant, who Scarlett had hired to work with their herd of cattle. Not only that, but he'd brought in a hundred head of dairy cows from his family's farm in Nevada when they'd lost a land rights battle in court, and there'd been talk of doing some cow cuddling classes.

Cache still wasn't fully on-board, and Scarlett was still trying to wrap her head around why someone would want to lay down in a messy field with a huge dairy cow. But whatever. The need to bring income into the ranch still remained a top priority—but no one would know it from the huge barbecue about to take place.

Adele had said she could make hamburgers and hot dogs gourmet, but she wouldn't reveal any of her plans to do such a thing. She'd asked Scarlett to provide the water-melon, and Jeri, the carpenter that had been hired to design and build the new dog enclosures, to bring a salad of some kind.

Jeri, Cache, and David all lived in the Community, and Scarlett's next hire was going to be an accountant. It was. It had to be. Scarlett couldn't keep up with the construction and the feeding schedule and Gramps's medical needs *and* maintain all the finances.

But for now, she cut watermelon and put the cubes in a bowl. The Internet radio station she had playing in the homestead changed to a new song—one Scarlett knew by heart. She started belting out the lyrics, though her singing voice wasn't going to win any awards.

Slice by slice and line by line, the watermelon got cut.

She put a lid on the bowl and sashayed her way over to the fridge to put the fruit away.

She yelled the last line of the song and pumped her fist high into the air. In the pause between songs, she heard laughter and then applause. Humiliation dove through her and she looked out the window to the back yard, where all the men were setting up for the picnic.

The open window.

They all stood there applauding, and rather than be worried about what any of them thought about her, Scarlett grinned and did a deep bow, the next song coming on the radio and drowning out their chuckles.

She laughed at herself as she started cleaning up the cutting board. She realized that she was definitely a different person standing in this kitchen than she'd been in the one in her small apartment in LA.

That woman would've never laughed at herself after an embarrassing incident. She wouldn't have bowed to those teasing her. She probably wouldn't have even been singing along and jamming out to a teenage pop song.

Scarlett liked this version of herself better, and a warm glow started down in her toes and rose through her bloodstream.

She finished cleaning up the kitchen and went outside. The heat seemed to radiate off the cement steps, but it was cooler on the grass and even better under the tent that had taken shape under Hudson's command.

"Have you seen Adele?" she asked.

He glanced toward the cabins several yards away. "Nope. But it smells amazing when you get close to her door." He looked at Carson. "What did you call it?"

"It's chili," he said. "My mother used to make it several times a year." Carson didn't look toward the cabin. Didn't pause in his movement of setting out chairs.

"She is doing hamburgers and hot dogs," Scarlett said. "Chili makes sense for the dogs."

At that moment, Adele's front door opened, and she poked her head out. She scanned the back yard, and when she caught Scarlett's eye, she motioned for her to come over.

"I've been summoned," Scarlett said. She walked away from the men, very aware that the open door had caught and hooked Carson's attention.

Adele ducked back inside as Scarlett closed the last few feet and went up the steps. "Hurry," she hissed from inside the house.

"Why?" Scarlett said, taking the steps two at a time and entering the house. She was barely all the way inside before Adele slammed the door closed. It definitely smelled like chili in here. And onions. And—"Did you make guacamole?"

She practically ran into the kitchen. "You did. Adele." She gazed lovingly at the condiment and then smiled at her friend. "Guacamole is my love language."

Adele rolled her eyes in a good-natured way. "I know,

sweetie." She reached over and tucked Scarlett's hair behind her ear. "How are things going with Hudson?"

"You gestured me wildly over here to ask about my boyfriend?"

"No, I wanted you to taste the chili and make sure it's not too hot." She opened a drawer and took out a spoon. "Wait, wait, wait." She adjusted the lighting on the bowl and pressed the button on the video camera. "All right, you'll get to be in one of the videos."

"Oh, so I'm a hand model now." Scarlett rather liked that, and she started to move the spoon toward the bowl again.

"Wait, wait," Adele said.

Scarlett glared at her, wondering if this was why Adele had made guacamole—so she could annoy Scarlett to death and not have any repercussions. "What?" she asked.

"You have to do it slowly. Slower than you think you need to. And then you're going to do the same thing with a fork and the hot dog." She pointed to the ready and waiting chili dog, which looked beautiful under the bright lights.

"Okay, slowly," Scarlett confirmed. She moved her spoon through the chili the slowest she ever had and tasted the chili. The flavor of cayenne and ground beef hit her first, then tomato and a little hint of something she couldn't name.

"Too hot?"

"It's the best chili in the world," Scarlett said. "And it's not too hot at all."

"Okay, hot dog." She moved it closer and nudged a bowl of cheese too. "It's a chili cheese dog. Okay, go."

Scarlett sprinkled cheese on the hot dog—slowly—and then cut off a bite with a fork. She didn't have to eat that, but she did, because if there was anything better than a chili cheese dog, she didn't want to know about it.

"Mm, Adele, you're a goddess."

"Okay, help me get all this stuff outside. And don't let anyone in." She picked up a crockpot full of chili, and she nodded toward the bag of cheese and a bag of hot dog buns. "We'll have to make a couple of trips to get the caramelized onions and other toppings for the burgers."

Scarlett did what her friend asked, making three trips to get all the condiments out to the serving table. Apparently they were going to have gourmet bacon burgers with melted Muenster cheese and caramelized onions, guacamole, and lightly grilled tomatoes.

Adele lit the grill and started getting things set up on the shelf connected to the appliance. Jeri arrived, and she was a bosomy brunette that had a quick wit and loads of personality.

"Heya," she said, carrying a huge white bowl. "Potato salad."

"You're kidding," Scarlett said.

"No." Jeri looked from Scarlett to Adele and back.

"She said I could make any side salad I wanted, and my mom has a killer potato salad recipe."

"No, no, it's fine," Scarlett said. "It's just my favorite." She grinned at Jeri. "And Adele made guacamole, which is also my favorite. I think you guys are trying to get me to gain weight." She laughed, glad when the others did too.

"Mm, then there would be more of you to love," Hudson said from behind her, snaking one hand around her waist.

"Oh, geez," Adele said under her breath, but Scarlett giggled as she turned into Hudson.

"Yeah, you know how I feel about that." She grinned up at him, because he was playfully smiling down at her. His statement was obviously banter, and Scarlett suddenly reminded herself that she wasn't alone with him.

She cleared her throat and stepped back. "Adele is making hamburgers to order, since there's only a few of us."

"You think eleven is a few?" Hudson asked.

"Few enough to make hamburgers to whatever temperature people want," Adele said, opening the lid on the grill. "So we're ready to start," she said to Scarlett. Then she opened a package of hot dogs and laid them onto the hot grill rack.

Then she faced the tables that had been set up as Scarlett said to Hudson, "You wanna whistle and get everyone over here?" The volunteers had set up a badminton net and a set of horseshoes in the shade along the side of the house, and they were playing over there.

Hudson puckered his lips and an ear-splitting whistle rent the air.

"Time to get started," Scarlett called, and everyone came over. She didn't know everyone well besides Adele, Carson, and Hudson, but she was getting to know them better. She hoped Last Chance Ranch would be a place they all could stay for a long, long time.

"Where's Gramps?" she asked, and Hudson flinched.

"Oh, my gosh. I forgot I said I'd go get him." He started across the lawn at a jog. "Start without me," he called over his shoulder.

Scarlett did, explaining the food and giving all the credit to Adele. "And I just wanted to say that I'm so glad each of you are here at Last Chance Ranch." She beamed around at everyone. "I'm really grateful for you, and...let's eat." So she needed to work on her sentimental speeches in her spare time.

No one seemed to mind her less-than-eloquent welcome to the picnic, and they started getting food. She went across the lawn to meet Gramps and Hudson, along with three dogs who seemed to be Gramps's shadows lately.

A sense of joy filled her as she kissed Gramps's forehead and said, "What do you want, Gramps? Hamburger or hot dog?"

A WEEK LATER, Scarlett paced in the kitchen as she drank a chocolate protein shake. Jewel had called a couple of hours ago, and she had that pair of dogs she'd mentioned when she'd first come to Last Chance Ranch and a paint pony that needed a new home.

Scarlett had agreed to take them instantly, and she was thrilled to have her first new adoptees on the ranch coming. Jewel had explained that the animals would come with their complete records, which included their veterinarian care as well as their names.

All her phone call had done was remind Scarlett that she still hadn't hired a volunteer coordinator, a veterinarian or any other animal health care professionals, or an accountant. So she'd have to look through their files and make sure they were healthy—Jewel had said they were—and assess any needs they may have by herself.

Which was probably okay. She should know how to do this stuff if she was going to run the ranch.

A dog barked at the same time she heard the crunch of tires in her driveway, and she hurried toward the front door. A navy blue truck sat there with a horse trailer attached to it. Two white dogs stood in the back, and Scarlett stared at them.

Jewel got out of the truck and moved to the dogs in the back, giving them both a little pat on the head. Scarlett couldn't believe what she was seeing.

"Come on, guys," Jewel said, and the two English retrievers whined to get out of the truck. Jewel made them wait as she lowered the tailgate, and then both dogs—Scarlett's dogs—jumped down from the truck and ran toward her.

Tears flowed down her face as she went down the steps to greet Billy and Bob, and she said, "Hey, babies. Hey, my puppies." They both licked her face, which made her laugh, and it was odd to be crying and laughing at the same time.

"Okay, so this is—"

"Billy," she said, stroking the dog's face with both of her hands. "And Bob." She let him lick her cheek, the way he'd done so many times before.

"Yeah," Jewel said. "How'd you know?"

Scarlett stood up and took the folder Jewel had extended toward her. "These were my dogs. I lost them in my divorce to my ex." She flipped open the folder, her eyes flying across the page there, but she wasn't exactly sure what she was looking for or where to find it.

"Your dogs?" Jewel asked.

"I can't believe Vance gave them to a shelter." She slapped the folder closed. "Why didn't he call me? I'd have taken them in a heartbeat." Of course he wouldn't call her. He'd fought her for two years to keep Billy and Bob with him. And the judge had agreed, because the paperwork was in Vance's name. The pet insurance too. The credit care card they used for veterinary bills.

So the judge had determined the dogs belonged to him. And only six months later, he'd given them to a shelter?

"We've only had them for a month," Jewel said. "And now they get to be here with you."

"I'm adopting them," she said quickly. "I can do that, right? Adopt them from Forever Friends?"

"Of course, Scarlett." Jewel put her hand on Scarlett's forearm. "So I guess we just need to get this horse over to his new home." She walked back toward the truck. "You didn't lose a horse in your divorce, did you?"

Scarlett laughed, but way down deep, something seethed. Anger. She could not believe Vance. She wanted to call him and scream at him, but she didn't have his number anymore. And even if she did, she wouldn't call him. Not even for this.

She rode with Jewel over to Horse Heaven, where Sawyer met them. He grinned and said, "Hey, ladies. What've we got here?"

"He's a paint," Jewel said. "Three years old. Good boy, but likes to kick a little."

Sawyer opened the horse trailer and expertly guided the animal out. "What's his name?"

"Blade," Jewel said, running her hand down the side of his neck. She obviously loved the horse, and while Scarlett had a soft spot for all animals, the bigger ones scared her a little bit still.

"Come on, Blade," Sawyer said. "I'm going to start him

in the pasture alone. See how he does." He led the horse away, and Scarlett could admit that it was beautiful.

"Thank you, Jewel," she said. She bent down to scratch behind Billy's ears.

"Of course," she said. "We'll probably have a few more dogs for you soon. We're doing our big adoption events every weekend until Labor Day, but any we can't find forever homes for, we'll need a new place for them."

"I can take them," she said. "As many as you've got. I hired a carpenter, and she's making great progress on the new enclosures."

"Yes, I think I'll swing over there and talk to her," Jewel said.

"All right," Scarlett said. "I'll contact Adrian for the adoption papers. I'm going to hire someone to do that here too. I just haven't gotten to it yet." There were so many things she hadn't gotten to.

"Oh, it's fine. Have you heard from Rich about the website?"

"Yes, he called last week. We went over everything, and we should be up soon. He said he'd email when it was live."

"All right then." Jewel exhaled. "I'm so glad you got your pups back." She got in her truck and drove away, leaving Scarlett to watch the dust settle—and reunite with her dogs.

She crouched down, her emotions overwhelming her again. She just couldn't believe they were here, and she straightened and said, "Come on, guys. There's someone you have to meet." And while it was mid-July and no one should be striding outside in a California summer, she did as she headed for Hudson's house.

Hudson—the person she wanted to share her good news with. And her bad news. And everything in between.

Chapter Sixteen

Hudson had just sat down to eat his turkey sandwich when someone banged on his door. He startled and Hound jumped to his feet—well, as much as the old dog could do. He looked at Hudson and then started for the door, a single bark coming out of his mouth. It sounded rusty and misused, because the dog literally never barked.

"Hudson?" Scarlett called, and Hudson got up from the table.

"C'mon in," he said, and the door opened a moment later.

He reached the doorway to find her standing there, crying. His pulse skipped like a perfectly thrown rock on still water. "What's wrong, sweetheart?" he asked in his most tender voice. He didn't dare move toward her as this situation was brand new and he had no idea how she'd react.

She pointed at the two dogs crowding into the doorway to get a better sniff at Hound. "These are my dogs," she said, her voice much too high. "Remember I told you I lost my fur babies in the divorce?"

"Yes," he said slowly, trying to put together the pieces.

"Jewel just brought them. Vance took them to the shelter about a month ago." She smiled amidst her tears and stepped into his house. "Can you believe this, Hudson? No one adopted them, and she brought them here." She wiped her tears, and she was lovely and beautiful and gentle with those tears coming down her face.

"Okay," he said, gathering her into his arms. She fit so well there, and Hudson felt her wedging herself right into his heart. If he wasn't careful, he was going to fall in love with her, this woman he held while she gripped his shoulders like she couldn't stand without him.

"This is good news, right?" he asked, and she pulled away enough to look at him.

"Yes, this is great news."

"So we're crying because we're happy."

She grinned and nodded, wiping her face again.

"I'm happy you're happy," he said, brushing his lips along her cheek. "So let's see who we've got here." He stepped away from her and greeted the dogs. They were good-looking dogs, and they didn't seem to be in ill health. He scratched behind their ears, smiling at them as their tongues hung out of their mouths. "And what are your names?"

"Billy and Bob," Scarlett said. "They're brothers. We got them—I mean, I wanted them, and Vance got them for me as a surprise."

"For a birthday?" Hudson asked.

"No, just because. That was one of the reasons I couldn't get them." She knelt down next to him and started rubbing the dogs too. "Vance said he bought them, and they were his. It didn't matter that I said they were a gift to me. I had no proof. He had the purchase documents." She shrugged, but Hudson could hear the hint of pain in her voice.

"I just can't believe it," she said. "It just feels surreal to me."

"So you don't need me over at the Canine Club to help with the new dogs, do you?"

She grinned as she shook her head. "No, these dogs are going to live with me."

Hudson liked seeing her so happy, but his gypsy soul wanted to get off the ranch for a few days. He'd been thinking about asking her to go with him. Where, he wasn't sure. He had the camper shell he could easily put back on the truck, and he could literally go anywhere he wanted.

His mouth turned dry, but the opportunity to ask her hovered between them.

"Hey, you okay?" she asked, putting one hand on

his arm.

He felt like she'd branded him, but he nodded anyway. "Yeah."

She went back to the dogs, and even Hound got a few pats. She jumped to her feet. "Gramps. Hey, guys, let's go meet Gramps." She started to step over the dogs to get to the front door, and Hudson found his chance to ask her to go on a road trip with him disappearing.

"Scarlett," he blurted before she could leave.

She turned back. "Yeah?"

"I was wondering...." He took his cowboy hat off and ran his hands through his hair. "I want to get off the ranch for a couple of days."

"You do?"

"Just a quick trip to the beach." As he spoke, he realized that was what he wanted to do. See the ocean up close. Hear the waves. Eat some seafood. "I was thinking maybe you'd like to come with me."

Her eyebrows shot up, and Hudson wanted to suck the words right back into his throat. She recovered quickly, and her eyes searched his face. "A trip," she finally said.

"A few days away from the stress of this place. From all the animals. The dogs can come, of course. But don't you want to just get away from things for a while?" Hudson felt the craving to get away clawing at him. And he wanted her to come too, because it would be good for her. Good for him to have her with him.

"I do, yeah," she said. "But I don't know if now's a good time."

"Okay, then when?" he asked.

She looked away, and he could tell she was just stalling. That she didn't want to come with him. "It's okay," he said. "You don't have to come. But I'm going to leave Friday, I think. Just head to the beach. Stay for a couple of days. I'll be back on Monday, so I won't be gone long. I'll talk to Sawyer about covering my animals."

He turned to go back to his sandwich, wishing his stomach wasn't so jittery. He really was hungry, and he had a full afternoon ahead of him out in the wilds.

"Do you go to church when you go on vacation?"

He glanced up at Scarlett, who'd followed him back into the cabin.

"If I feel like it," he said. "Sometimes the vacation is a way back to God, you know?"

She pulled out the second chair at the table and sat down. "I'd like to go with you. I think I can leave on Friday and come back on Monday."

"Really?" His eyes searched hers. "It's fine if you don't want to. Honestly."

"Do you have enough room in that truck for two people to sleep?"

"Yeah, you can have the camper shell, and I'll sleep in the backseat."

She laughed. "Hudson, honey, there's no way you can sleep on that backseat. It's tiny, and well, you're not."

"Are you calling me fat?" he asked, hoping she wouldn't be offended.

She smiled and shook her head. "Broad-shouldered."

"More of me to love," he said, rolling those shoulders she was talking about.

"Stop it."

"Well, I don't want you to sleep in the backseat. The camper shell has a nice bed. I can set up a tent on the beach."

"We'll work it out," she said.

"Yeah," he said. "It'll work out."

"Great." She stood up and stepped around the table before leaning down and pressing her lips to his. She kissed him in a slow, passionate way that said all kinds of things he didn't understand.

When she pulled away, he reached for her again and brought her back. He kissed her again, definitely feeling himself falling in love with her. He didn't even try to stop himself, because he liked this ranch. He liked the peacefulness of life here. He liked Scarlett.

Yeah, he *really* liked Scarlett.

HUDSON TIGHTENED the cinch strap and led a horse named Trixie out of the stables. He and Trixie had bonded over the weeks, and she'd simply listen to him as they rode around the perimeter of the ranch to map it.

The task took time, sure, but it was something Hudson enjoyed. He had a notebook and he put features of the land, buildings, piles of wood, anything he saw, on the map that was coming together.

Today, Carson and Sawyer had horses saddled up too, and Hudson was the last to swing up onto his animals and say, "Okay."

The three of them set out, Trixie half a step ahead, as the others hadn't come on all the mapping expeditions. The stress of the morning melted away though the sun was hot. He'd packed plenty of water, and his cowboy hat kept his face shaded.

"I'm headed off the ranch for a few days this weekend," he said. "Can you two cover my responsibilities with the horses and llamas?"

"Off the ranch?" Sawyer asked. "Where you goin'?"

"Just to the beach," Hudson said. "The ocean clears my head."

"I'm sure we can cover it," Carson said.

"Thanks." Hudson let Trixie take a few more plodding steps, trying to decide what he wanted to say. Sawyer had moved into the cabin in the back beside Carson, and the three of them had gotten along really great over the past several weeks. These were his friends, and Hudson took a moment to enjoy that realization.

"Scarlett's comin'," he said.

Silence prevailed for a few more strides. "So you two must be getting along great," Carson said.

"Well enough," Hudson said.

"Must be serious if you're going on a trip together."

Hudson thought about Carson's words. He and Scarlett were dating. They weren't seeing anyone else. His blood heated and threatened to boil him alive if he didn't kiss her every day.

"He can't even confirm it," Sawyer said. "Must be *really* serious."

"It's...been about eight weeks," Hudson said. "So it's still new." That was why his feelings for the woman were so strong. He knew they'd settle. Had experienced such things before.

But with Scarlett, it sure was taking a long time to get his hormones under control. He kissed her like every time was the last time, and he needed to start acting his age—which would go up another number in just a few weeks.

He found the grove of oak trees, said, "Ho," to get Trixie to stop, and pulled out the notebook from the saddlebag behind him. "Okay, so I've got this grove here." He flipped pages until he found the section of the ranch they were currently on. "We stick here and go west until we get to the cemetery."

"There's a cemetery out here?" Sawyer asked.

"I think it's for the animals," he said. "The headstones are interesting. Only first names on most of them. A few say things like, 'Beloved companion to Ben.'"

"Interesting," Sawyer said. "Have you told Scarlett about it?"

"Not yet." She wanted a presentation of the land once it was all mapped, and Hudson added it to the list of things he hadn't brought up with her yet. Like his birthday. Like if she might want to adopt after they got married. Like marriage, which should probably come before a discussion about adoption. Like his strengthening feelings for her.

He couldn't believe he was even considering marrying someone else. When Jan had left and he'd sold his shop, he'd determined to do something different with his life. He traded in wrenches and oil-stained hands for the nomad's life, and now he wore a cowboy hat and boots every day.

The man he was now, riding atop a horse, felt more authentic than who he'd been before. A memory from his childhood flashed through his mind, and he knew it was the Lord reminding him that his family was only twenty minutes up the road and he should probably go see them.

Soon, he told himself. *After this weekend at the beach.*

"So I asked Adele to lunch," Sawyer said.

"Oh, boy," Carson said, and Hudson looked back and forth between them. "What did she do? Slam the door in your face? Roll her eyes?"

Sawyer looked at him. "She said yes."

"What?" Carson's shock permeated the air, and Hudson squirmed in his saddle. He knew the cowboy from Montana had a king-sized crush on the blonde in the middle cabin. Sawyer obviously didn't know that, or he wouldn't have asked her out.

Sawyer shrugged. "She actually said it would be nice to get off the ranch for a meal or two."

"I've asked her to dinner at least five times," Carson said. He looked at Hudson. "What in the world?"

"I don't know," Hudson said at the same time Sawyer said, "I didn't know you liked her, Carson. I'm sorry."

"I *don't* like her," Carson said darkly. "I only follow her around like a lovesick puppy, doing every single thing she barks at me." He continued to mutter under his breath, and Sawyer exchanged a guilty look with Hudson.

"Are you thinking you and Scarlett will ever get married?" he asked, and Hudson dang near fell out of his saddle.

"Wow, I'm really saying all the wrong things today, aren't I?" Sawyer gazed off into the distance. "Maybe I'll just head back in."

"It's fine," Hudson said, blowing out his breath. "I don't know what will happen. I'm not looking to tie the knot any time soon."

"Because of Jan."

"Yeah," he said, wishing that woman didn't get to inflict herself on his life when she wasn't even around anymore. "Because of Jan." And because Scarlett didn't seem ready to take that step either.

He kept his eyes moving left and right, looking for items to map. Or was he looking for an answer to Sawyer's question? He didn't think he'd find it imprinted on the waving grasses on the ranch. Or even the ocean waves.

But he threw up a prayer to God to know what to do about Scarlett, and when, because he sure liked having her in his life.

But permanently? His last name after her first?

Now that, he didn't know. But maybe the Lord would whisper the answer to him that weekend, as he listened to the waves roar ashore.

Chapter Seventeen

"I can't believe I'm so nervous." Scarlett ran her hands down her stomach, which wasn't anywhere near flat. "The beach. I can't go to the beach with him."

Adele tucked a black swimming suit into Scarlett's suitcase. "Of course you can. You've already said yes, and you're leaving in an hour." She gave Scarlett a pointed look she barely felt. "Which is why you should've let me come help you pack last night."

"I didn't sleep at all last night," Scarlett said, all of her senses so heightened she could barely use them. "This is a bad idea, right?" She met Adele's eye, and she sighed and sat down on the bed beside the suitcase.

"Come sit for a second."

Scarlett complied, but only because she didn't know what else to do.

"Honey, you like this man, right?"

"Yes."

"And he likes you."

Scarlett thought about the way he held her close to his heart, the way he kissed her like he needed her to survive. "Yes," she whispered.

"Then just let go of whatever fear is brewing inside you and go have fun."

"But the swimming suit—"

"Girl, he's seen you. He's touched your waist and arms and if he doesn't know what you've got by now, he's blind."

"I don't think he's blind," Scarlett said.

Adele laughed and shook her head. "Of course he isn't. Scarlett, you are what you are. Your body is beautiful, and Hudson knows it."

Scarlett appreciated the words, as well as the sentiment behind them. She clenched her fingers together and then released them. "You're right."

"Of course I'm right." Adele looked at the suitcase. "Okay, pajamas. I don't think we've put those in yet." She started to get up, but Scarlett put her hand on Adele's arm.

"Why are you going out with Sawyer instead of Carson?"

"I—" Adele snapped her mouth shut, her eyes widening instead. She searched Scarlett's face, clearly trying to come up with a reasonable explanation. But Scarlett didn't think she had one.

Her shoulders slumped and she finally said, "He's not in the plan, you know? You're the one who runs off and does things willy-nilly. I'm the planner, remember?" Her eyes begged Scarlett to understand, to reassure her that what she was doing was right.

"You can't plan your whole life," Scarlett said.

"Yes, I can." Adele stood up, this conversation clearly over. "Now, do you want something a little sexier for pajamas, or are we going with the middle-aged woman look?"

"I'm too old to try for sexy," Scarlett said, causing Adele to scoff and wave her hand.

"Rubbish. You're never too old for sexy." She stepped over to Scarlett's dresser and opened the top drawer. "Oh, these will do nicely." She turned, grinned, and put the pajamas in Scarlett's suitcase. Another item off her checklist. Another plan completed.

Scarlett thanked her friend and hugged her before Adele slipped out the back door so Scarlett would be alone when Hudson arrived to pick her up. Her stomach buzzed again once she only had herself for company.

"What are you doing?" she whispered to herself as she paced toward the front door. She touched it and turned around, walking the other way now. At least she'd get in some steps before their road trip started. Burn off some excess calories before he took her for fish and chips—an idea he'd texted that morning.

Her thoughts lingered on Adele, and why she couldn't just add Carson to her list. She almost texted the suggestion to her, but the sound of a heavy vehicle on gravel met her ears. She spun back toward the front door, her heart hurling itself against her ribcage like it was trying to get free.

A knock sounded, and the door opened. Everything seemed like it was happening in slow motion, and Scarlett couldn't move. Then Hudson's broad shoulders and tall frame filled the doorway. His face filled with a smile, and he said, "Hey, beautiful," like their trip would be the easiest thing he did that week.

The sound of his voice also thawed her, and she crossed the room to him. "Hey." She stretched up and kissed him quickly, deciding to get the confessions out early. "I'm so nervous."

"Are you?" He reached for her suitcase and picked it up, pausing before he left the house. "Why?"

"I don't know." Her fingers started winding around each other. "Aren't you nervous?"

"No," he said. "I'm excited, though. We've been working way too hard on this ranch."

"I like working hard on the ranch."

"I do too," he said. "Honestly, I do. But everyone needs a break sometimes." He still didn't turn to go outside. "Scarlett, what's really going on?"

"Nothing," she said. "I just...I haven't—I'm—are we moving too fast?" Scarlett hadn't been able to pinpoint the source of her anxiety, but she thought it might be simply because she wasn't ready for a serious relationship.

Hudson blinked at a normal rate, his eyes locked on

hers. "I don't think so, but I respect your feelings. If this is too fast for you, that's fine."

"I don't know what's too fast for me," she said. Something clawed at her insides. "I just...." She exhaled. "I'm ruining it, aren't I?"

"Not at all," he said easily, like they were talking about the weather. But he didn't say anything else. Just stood there, looking handsome and exuding confidence, strength, and peace.

Scarlett seized onto his demeanor, determined to be as confident, strong, and secure as he was. "All right." She drew in a deep breath and straightened. "I want to go."

"Do you?" He peered at her, even leaning a little closer. "I don't want you to come if you're uncomfortable."

"Discomfort makes us grow," she said. "My mother always told me that. Not that I need any help with the growing, the way Adele is making sweets these days." She gave a nervous giggle that contradicted her determination to be calm. "She says the foodie market has really developed a sweet tooth lately."

Hudson flashed a smile that she barely saw it exited so fast. "I don't like it when you put yourself down," he said, finally taking the steps out the front door. "I'll just leave this here until you figure out what you want to do." With that, he walked away, lifting his hat and running his free hand through his hair, something she'd only seen him do when he was nervous—or frustrated.

Scarlett's insides now felt like someone had frozen

them and then smashed them with a hammer. Sharp shards stabbed her, and she couldn't get a full breath.

I don't like it when you put yourself down.

You're the one who runs off and does things willy-nilly.

Was she? She'd dated Vance for over a year before they'd even talked about a future together. He'd never minded when she called herself overweight or whale-like. Of course, when they'd met and then married, she weighed about sixty pounds less than she did now. But as she put on the weight, he never said she was beautiful. In fact, he usually laughed when she went down the self-deprecation route.

Hudson's truck started, and Scarlett had a very scary moment where she thought he'd leave without her. And that answered all of her fears and doubts.

She didn't want him to leave without her.

Without wasting another moment, she ducked out of the house, pulled the door closed behind her, and grabbed her suitcase. He saw her coming and got out of the truck, nervousness in his eyes but his mouth spreading into a smile.

"I never gave you a tour of the camper shell," he said, taking her bag from her. "And this is going back there, so do you want the grand tour?"

"Yes," she said, watching him as he looked away from her. She wanted to apologize, this tension between them unwelcome.

He moved to the back of the truck and typed in a four-digit code.

"Fancy," she said. "Do I get to know that?"

"Zero-eight-zero-four," he said. "It's my birthday." Their eyes locked again while surprise rose through Scarlett.

"Like, August?" That was only a few weeks away, and Scarlett's party-planning gene kicked into gear.

"Yes," he said. "Like August fourth." He opened the door and pulled down a set of two steps. "Okay, so this is the front door." He went up the steps and into the back of the truck, which somehow accommodated his height.

"There's a shower right here," he said. "I didn't use it much, because you have to have water hookups and an outflow. But bathing is possible." He pointed to his left. "Closet here. We'll put your bag in there."

He moved further into the camper, and she followed him, marveling at the built-in shower. "Is the water hot?"

"It has a twenty-gallon tank," he said. "It's good for one person, and then you have to wait a bit." He gestured to the two-burner stovetop and sink on his left. "Kitchen here. Has a microwave and fridge. That's what I mainly use when I'm on the road." He turned but couldn't take a step because of the table immediately on his right. "We eat here. Lots of seating. Step there up to the bed. That's the part that hangs over the cab."

"This is so nice," Scarlett said. "What kind of wood is

this?" She ran her fingers along the wall above the kitchen sink.

"Cedar," he said.

"I had no idea it was all of this." She smiled as she looked around. "You have everything you need in here."

"No toilet," he said.

"Well, besides that." She linked her arm through his, and he turned sideways. That was all he could do, as the space between the chest-high sink and hotplate and the dining room table was only wide enough for one person. "I love this."

"Yeah?" He looked at her out of the corner of his eye.

Scarlett wondered if those words could morph into *I love you,* and another tremor of fear ran through her. She tipped up to kiss his cheek, and said, "Yeah, this is so great."

"It's a comfortable enough bed," he said.

"I'm sure it'll be fine." She eyed the step like it might try to do her a personal wrong. "I don't know if I can get up there." It certainly wouldn't allow her to stand upright, and she'd have to sort of flop over into the bed.

"Sure, you can," he said. "And we'll park somewhere by a bathroom."

"Are you saying I can't go all night without going to the bathroom?" she asked playfully. "Because if you are, you would be right." And the thought of getting up and getting down out of the bed, going outside to a public bathroom...well, it didn't really appeal to Scarlett.

She turned and moved the few steps to the door and down the steps. "And you lived in this for a year, right?"

"About thirteen months," he said. "Went all the way up to the Canadian border and all the way down to Mexico."

"Hmm." She waited with him while he put up the steps and then closed and locked the door. "Looking for something?"

"Yeah," he said, looking at her. "I was."

"And did you find it?" She laced her fingers through his, all worries about how fast they were moving in their relationship gone.

"I'm not sure yet," he said, looking over her shoulder at something in the sky. "I will say that I sure like being here at Last Chance Ranch." Their eyes met again, and he added, "With you."

Warmth filled Scarlett, and her heart started doing that pounding, twisting thing. "You just know all the right things to say, don't you?" She giggled and stretched up to kiss him, glad he leaned down to make her job easier.

He kissed her tenderly, unlike some of the more passionate kisses they'd shared. She liked the ones where he pressed her into the door behind her, seemingly unable to get close enough to her. And the ones where he held her face in both of his hands, like he treasured her so much he had to keep her right in front of him.

This tender, slow kiss shot into first place, though, because she felt something in it. She felt loved.

She pulled away and licked her lips, tasting him there. "Mm," she said. "Shouldn't we go?"

"Oh, look who's in a hurry now." He chuckled and tucked her into his side as he took her to the passenger door. He opened it but didn't move out of the way. "And Scarlett? The things I say aren't just pretty words."

She could drown in the depths of his dark eyes. "Yeah, I know," she said. He stepped to the side and helped her into the truck, closing the door behind her and walking around the back instead of the front.

And she did know that what Hudson said, he meant. After all, he wasn't particularly loquacious, and a man of few words had to mean every one he said.

Scarlett smiled to herself and scooted over on the seat to sit right next to her boyfriend. With this being their first road trip together, Scarlett didn't want to miss a thing.

Chapter Eighteen

Hudson kept one hand on the wheel and one in Scarlett's. He didn't want to admit that yes, maybe he was a little nervous. Being in the camper shell with her had shown him how tiny it was, and that there was no way he could sleep in there with her.

He'd been entertaining the idea of putting down the kitchen table and laying down the bench seats where he normally ate or did crossword puzzles. But that was only a step forward and a step up to the divinely smelling Scarlett, and he didn't think he could lay there and fall asleep with her so close.

She hummed along to the radio as he drove, getting used to the extra weight and bulk of the camper shell again. The beach was only about an hour and a half away, and he'd chosen Huntington Beach, because the sand was warm and while it was sometimes windy, they had great facilities.

He'd told himself that if the lodging was a problem, they'd simply find a hotel. She could sleep upstairs in the room, and he'd take the camper shell in the parking lot. Plus, that way, he'd have a place to park. As he thought about it again, he concluded that a hotel was probably the best option.

"What do you think about getting a hotel?" he asked.

She looked at him, her fingers twirling around that piece of hair she favored. "A hotel?"

"I think you'd be more comfortable."

"I'm fine in the camper shell."

"Fine, I'd be more comfortable."

The weight of her gaze on the side of his face did little to ease his nerves. "Can we afford a hotel?"

"Of course we can," he said, glancing at her. "There may be something I haven't told you yet."

"Oh, a secret." She smiled, and Hudson did too.

"I didn't need to live in my truck for thirteen months. I did it to get out of Santa Monica. Cut ties completely. I told you I sold the mechanic shop and bought the truck." He shifted slightly in his seat, because discussing money made him uncomfortable. "I worked odd jobs for the time I lived in the camper. I only used what I earned to pay for food and gas and other expenses."

"Are you saying you're good with money?"

"I mean, I guess." He looked at her. "I can set and follow a budget."

He couldn't truly see her eyes behind her sunglasses, and the traffic in front of him suddenly braked. He did too, gripping the wheel as the truck and shell took an extra few seconds to slow down. An accident avoided, he said, "I sold my mechanic shop for over five million dollars. I haven't touched a dime of it, besides paying for this outfit."

He could see her eyes widen beneath those lenses. "You're kidding."

"I'm not."

"Jan didn't take any of it?"

"Jan took plenty," he said, not really wanting to get into everything Jan had taken with her when she'd left. He waited for the flash of pain to come, the resentment, the anger. Only a tiny flicker of a flame licked against his heart, and it was only made of fury. Fine, maybe a touch of resentment too.

But no pain.

He didn't have time to wonder at that, because Scarlett asked, "How much do you have left?"

"All of it," he said. "I only had to give Jan ten percent, because she ran her own business from our home, and she got to keep that." The day he'd moved out was one of the worst of his life, and once again, he waited for the tortuous memories to flood his mind.

They didn't. Sure, he felt sadness, but mostly because there was still an inkling of missing his previous life. He'd been comfortable, in a nice house overlooking the ocean. His own business that made great money. Work he loved. A wife he adored.

He cleared his throat, wishing the thoughts could be cleansed as easily. "Do you ever miss your old life?" he asked, realizing he'd just changed the subject rapidly.

Scarlett looked away from him, the only answer he needed. But she said, "Yeah, I mean, I guess."

"I do," he said. "And not because I want it back. It's just...that was my life for a long time. I remember being happy in it."

"Yeah," she said, a wistful quality to her voice. "I loved my cramped apartment in the city."

"Let's drive by it," he said, the idea just occurring to him. "And on the way back on Monday, we'll take the long way up to Santa Monica, and I'll show you my shop and my house." He looked at her. "You want to?"

She didn't want to, he could tell. His enthusiasm waned, and he said, "Okay, dumb idea."

"I like this life I have now," she said. "I've always loved the ranch, and I like myself so much better now than who I was in LA."

"Can't argue with you there," he said.

"How have you changed?" she asked.

"Well, I found God in my thirteen months on the road. I learned to enjoy simple things like sunrises and hot coffee. A warm shower. Running water."

She laughed lightly and pulled out her phone. "I bet

you did." She held her phone up and pointed it at them. "Let's take a picture."

"I'm driving."

"The traffic is barely moving. Come on." She nestled her shoulder back into his chest, and he had no choice but to grin at her phone. *Click, click, click*, and she lowered her arm. She grinned at the screen, and said, "Wow, my boyfriend is so handsome."

"Yeah?" He looked at her, more confessions piling up behind his tongue. "Listen," he started. "When I said back at the ranch that I didn't like it when you put yourself down—" He stopped when she abandoned her device to look at him. "I didn't mean to be rude. I just—I think you're gorgeous, and I'm kind of hoping you only packed bathing suits."

She blinked a couple of times before throwing her head back and laughing. "Hudson, I packed way more than bathing suits."

"Well, that's terrible news."

She continued to giggle as she tapped and swiped on her phone. "Sending this to you," she said, and a moment later, his phone chimed. She tucked it back into her pocket, laced her arm through his, and laid against his bicep. "I sure do like you, Hudson Flannigan. Did you pack more than swim trunks?"

"Not much more."

"Mm, I can't wait to get to the beach."

Hudson couldn't either, and he faced the red brake

lights in front of him, frustrated with city traffic for the first time in a long time.

A couple of hours later, he emerged from the camper shell wearing his swim gear, which consisted of a pair of swimming trunks, a ball cap, and a towel thrown over one arm. "You can change now," he said to Scarlett, who sat at the metal picnic table he'd parked beside.

She rose slowly, reached up and pushed her sunglasses down her nose to peer at him over the top of them. "Are you serious right now?"

"What?" He glanced down at his bare chest. "We're going into the ocean. I want to see that bathing suit."

She hastily pushed her glasses back into position and crossed her arms. "I don't know, Hudson."

"What don't you know?"

"Why do you like me?" she asked instead of answering his question.

"Because you're smart," he said. "And beautiful. And you have a big heart, which cares about hundreds of animals, and people, and Gramps." His mouth felt dry. She'd never really said it was okay he'd told her not to put herself down.

So she carried around a few extra pounds. He liked them. Found her sexy and stunning, and his fantasies and dreams were things he could never do until they were married.

And there was that M-word again. Hudson really

needed to get some things straight in his head. Number one, Scarlett was nowhere near a marriage discussion, which meant he couldn't be thinking about it either. Number two, if she needed time, he needed to give it to her.

"I'm going to go change," she said, marching away from him like he'd said something wrong. She went inside the camper shell, and he heard her suitcase hit the floor as she pulled it out of the closet.

He sighed and wiped his forehead. He'd put sunscreen on all the exposed skin, drank a whole bottle of water, and wandered down the shoreline and back, and Scarlett still hadn't come out of the camper shell.

"Scarlett?" he asked, rapping lightly on the door.

"I can't come out," she said.

"Then I'll come in."

"No," she called, but he'd already opened the door and committed to taking the steps. She couldn't hide in the camper shell; there wasn't anywhere to go. She stood before him in a black swimming suit that showed all her curves.

His heart bounced around inside his chest, and he said, "Wow, you're beautiful."

"You can't possibly think that."

"I absolutely think that." He took a step forward and laced his fingers through hers. "And I'll say it every day until you believe it." He bent down and kissed her, going slow and letting her set the pace.

When she finally pulled away, he said, "Come on. Let's go sit on the beach."

She came with him, grabbing a towel from the closet as he led her down the steps. With the camper shell locked and their beach bags with them, they walked through the sand in silence.

He set up their umbrella while she unfolded the chairs they'd rented from a surf shop. With her oversized bag between them, Hudson stretched his legs out in front of him and took her hand.

"I love the beach," he said. "My mother used to bring us when Dad got in a foul mood over something."

"What would he get upset about?"

"Horses," Hudson said. "Clients. Me." He hated that the old feelings still existed inside him. But they did, and he knew he needed to deal with them. "I think I'm going to go visit them next week."

"You are?"

They hadn't spoken about his parents much. A little here and there. Next week seemed way too soon for a visit. "Maybe for my birthday."

"No," she said, a hint of a whine in her voice. "I've been planning a party for you on your birthday."

His eyebrows quirked, and he looked at her. "You have? When?"

"You thought I was asleep on the way down here, didn't you?"

"You *were* asleep."

She giggled and squeezed his fingers. "Nope, I was party planning with my eyes closed." She sat up straight and said, "So definitely go visit them. But not on your birthday." She leaned over and kissed him, a devilish grin on her face. "I want you on your birthday."

"Oh, I see how it is," he said, but nothing could be further from the truth. He had no idea what she meant by "I want you."

He knew it wasn't in terms like *fiancé* and *groom*.

And that's not okay?

He thought about it as she settled back in her seat and the only sound between them became the roar of the waves as they washed ashore. In the end, it was okay that she wasn't ready for the next step in their relationship.

It had to be, because he could only see this relationship with her ending in one of two ways. Either they'd get married and be blissfully happy for the rest of their lives. Or she'd break up with him, he'd have to leave Last Chance Ranch, and he'd never see her again.

He was really hoping for the first scenario, and really all she needed was time. And Hudson had plenty of that to give.

So why did it feel like he was suddenly trapped between a rock and a hard place?

Chapter Nineteen

S carlett lay on the foam mattress in the camper shell, the darkness around her almost suffocating. Hudson had made a bed in the back of the truck, claiming he'd put all the seats down and it was plenty wide for his shoulders.

She hadn't been able to go look at it. Guilt would've had her offering him the bed again, and he'd have refused, and the awkwardness that had accompanied them on this road trip would've come back

She also didn't want to suggest a hotel, though that would've been her first choice. She couldn't afford it, and she didn't want Hudson to pay for it. *Five million dollars.*

The man had money, and while that didn't affect how she felt about him, it certainly changed things.

Don't put yourself down.

You're so beautiful.

I'll say it every day until you believe me.

Scarlett wanted to believe him, but something inside her wouldn't let her. She knew she couldn't continue a relationship with him without getting over this negative view she had of herself. She couldn't survive another marriage where she worried constantly if she was good enough for her husband, where she was paranoid every time he left the house.

To her knowledge, Vance had not cheated on her. But the fear was real that Hudson would find someone who "suited him better" the way Vance had done. Hudson hadn't said he felt like their relationship had stalled, but his actions suggested he felt it.

Scarlett hadn't felt it until he'd asked her to go on the road trip with him. Then every insecurity and doubt she'd had had reared up and plagued her day and night. Sitting beside him—a handsome, tan, strong man—in a bathing suit had been torture, and she'd made an excuse about an itchy tag after only forty-five minutes on the beach. She'd come back to the camper shell and changed into a pair of cutoffs and a tank top, which didn't cover much more of her body, but also didn't stick to all the wrong parts in such offensive ways.

He'd gone swimming in the ocean while she'd just waded out and laughed at him. They'd wandered down the beach until they found a stand selling corndogs and chips. They'd talked about his family a little more, and the ranch, and what Scarlett's dreams for it were.

And now she lay in a bed that smelled like him, and he

was approximately five feet below her in the cab. And she couldn't fall asleep.

She pulled out her phone and texted Adele. Something easy like, *Hey, just checking in. How are Billy and Bob?*

They'd decided to leave the dogs with Gramps and Adele, and both had seemed happy about the dog-sitting arrangements.

They're great, Adele sent back. *No pictures until I hear how things went with Hudson on the beach.*

Scarlett sighed, unsure of how to answer. She was a grown adult, and she didn't need to spill everything that happened in her relationship to her best friend.

You're second-guessing yourself again, aren't you? Adele knew her so well, which made Scarlett smile. But it wasn't even a happy smile, just one borne from nostalgia.

Maybe, she texted back.

Why can't you believe he likes you?

Scarlett didn't know. She said that, and then said, *Please send me a picture of the pups.*

One came in, and Adele mercifully didn't ask her any more questions. In fact, her next text after a picture of Scarlett's dogs was, *So I finally accepted a date with Carson. We went to lunch and then he kissed me.*

Scarlett sat straight up in bed, almost knocking her head against the top of the camper shell. "What?" she said out loud. She hit call on her phone, needing to talk to Adele right now.

Her best friend had been so adamant about her dislike of Carson, and she'd been strict in her no-boyfriend-at-the-ranch policy. And now she'd kissed the cowboy?

She didn't answer, instead sending her call to voice-mail, and Scarlett hung up without leaving a message. A text came in that said, *He's still here. Can't talk. I'll call you in the morning.*

"Still there?" Scarlett checked the time, and it was almost midnight. She grinned and shook her head. "Good luck, Adele," she whispered into the darkness, plugging in her phone, and lying back down.

This time, sleep took her quickly, and she dreamt of herself and Hudson. They wore their best clothes, and he danced with her under twinkling lights on the ranch. He laughed and leaned down, his love for her absolutely beautiful in the way he kissed her and held her right against his chest.

THE NEXT MORNING, she woke with light streaming through the windows in the camper shell. She and Hudson had never agreed on a time to get up and get going, but she swung her legs over the side of the bed quickly, not wanting him to be waiting for her.

She got down out of the sleeping quarters and opened her suitcase. She'd changed out of her pajamas and into a pair of shorts and a tank top before her phone rang.

"Adele," she said instead of hello. "What in the world is going on?"

"So maybe he's a nice guy," Adele said, also bypassing the greetings. "And maybe just because he's rich doesn't mean he's a jerk-face."

Scarlett laughed, the sound filling and bouncing around the camper. "Well, I'm glad. The tension between you two was almost too much to take."

"Oh, it was not." Adele scoffed. "Gramps has all the dogs today, by the way. We've got three goat yoga sessions, so we'll be busy all day."

"Oh, I'm sure you will," Scarlett teased.

Adele giggled and then said, "So what about you and Hudson? What's on the agenda for today?"

"No agenda," Scarlett said.

"And you're okay with that?"

"I mean, it's just a weekend."

"You live by a schedule," Adele said.

"That's you, sweetie," Scarlett said. "Lists and plans and all of that. I can just fly free for a weekend."

Adele laughed. "Yeah, but it'll drive you nuts. I mean, it's almost eight. Have you eaten yet?"

"As a matter of fact, I'm making breakfast now." She bent to open the mini-fridge and pulled out a container of eggs. "Bagel breakfast sandwiches."

"Who's the planner now?" Adele asked playfully.

Scarlett rolled her eyes and scoffed. "Oh, go kiss your new cowboy boyfriend."

"Cowboy *billionaire* boyfriend," Adele corrected. She laughed and said, "All right, I have to go check on the goats before our session. Scarlett, just promise me one thing."

"What's that?" She fiddled with the dials on the burners, pleased when one burst to life.

"Promise me you won't get too far inside your head," she said.

"I don't even know what that means," Scarlett said.

"It means that you worry too much about things that don't matter."

"Okay, gotta go," Scarlett said, and she hung up a moment later. She did *not* worry too much about things that didn't matter. If she worried about something, it mattered. It mattered a whole lot—to her.

"Adele's the one with triple locks on her cabin," Scarlett muttered to herself as she cracked eggs into the pan and scrambled them into round patties that would fit perfectly on the bagels.

She stuck a plate of ham into the microwave and pulled out the rest of the groceries she needed for the sandwiches. Butter, cream cheese, knives, and a tomato. Item by item, she moved the food out to the picnic table, glancing toward the front of the truck, almost expecting to see Hudson standing there.

He wasn't, but her heart still fluttered around inside her chest. She was in so deep with him already, and she wanted to take several steps backward for reasons she couldn't explain.

Then he came walking up the beach, those sexy board shorts falling to his knee and his gray T-shirt stretching across his chest wonderfully. And she wanted to accelerate their relationship. Really slam her foot on the gas pedal and see how far they could go.

Her feelings felt like they were riding a roller coaster, and she had no idea what she was doing with Hudson. She did know how to lay out food and make a bagel breakfast sandwich, so she focused on that.

After all, her relationship with Hudson was new, and she still had time to figure things out with him.

Didn't she?

She glanced at him, noticing the soft look on his face, and she wondered if she was already in love with him.

Absolute fear hit her hard, but she still managed to say, "Good morning," as she nudged the plate of tomatoes into place.

Chapter Twenty

Hudson woke before the sun, the flat light of near-dawn one of his favorite times of the day. Especially at the beach, where the air was always full of sound and life. He hadn't slept particularly well on the leather seats of the truck, but he could take a nap later.

The camper shell had air conditioning, and he'd find somewhere he could park for an hour or two. Maybe Scarlett would like to go shopping or something while he slept. The point was, they didn't have a plan and they didn't need one.

He drew in a deep breath of the early morning air and stretched his arms above his head. Then his back, and finally his legs, before walking down to the water's edge. He hadn't heard anything above him during the night, and he hoped Scarlett had slept well.

When he got back from his stroll along the sand, Scarlett had breakfast on the table. She glanced at him, a smile on her pretty face. "Good morning."

A flood of love filled him, and no matter how he tried to push it away, it wouldn't go. He took her easily into his arms, smiling at the way she giggled. He kissed her. Kissed her as deeply as he dared out in public and without wanting to scare her away.

"Now it is," he said when he finally pulled away. He surveyed the spread on the table. "What is all this?"

"Bagels," she said. "I warmed up some ham and made some eggs, so we can make breakfast sandwiches." She wore a hint of pride in her voice. "And I was thinking...." She reached for a bagel and spread some cream cheese on it.

He knew he'd made a good move when he'd asked her to plan the food. "What were you thinking?" His mouth watered, and he was thinking he needed to eat quickly so he could get back to kissing her.

"How far are we from Disneyland?"

Hudson almost dropped his bagel. "Disneyland?" He forked up a couple of pieces of ham. "I thought we were relaxing this weekend."

"We are." She glanced at him. "You don't find Disneyland relaxing?"

"On a Saturday in July? Sweetheart, that's the opposite of relaxing."

She laughed, finished making her sandwich, and said, "Yeah, you're right. It was a dumb idea."

"It's not a dumb idea," he said. "It's just...not what I thought this weekend was going to be." He could adjust, he supposed, but he was thinking more about riding the Ferris wheel on the pier, and greasy food that didn't cost an arm and a leg, and parking on the beach, not in a huge lot with Mickey ears on the signs.

She moved around the side of the table and sat with her back to him, facing the ocean as she ate. He joined her, disliking the awkwardness between them. Slowly, it leaked away, and Hudson didn't know what to say.

He hated feeling like this. When he'd first found out about Jan, he'd felt the exact same way. What to say? What to do? How to react? He had no idea, and he sighed.

"Look, Scarlett, maybe we should just go back to the ranch today."

"What? Why?"

Hudson was obviously misreading some things from her. "I don't know what I'm doing wrong."

"You're not doing anything wrong." She took a bite of her sandwich, a definite cold vibe coming from her.

"Then what's going on?"

She finished her breakfast and wiped her hands on a paper towel. "I'm scared."

"Of what? Me?"

"Us," she said. "I'm—I don't—"

Hudson watched the water, his stomach dropping with every moment where she didn't finish her sentence. Finally, he said, "I shouldn't have asked you on this trip."

He folded his arms and tried to unclench his jaw. "I'm sorry, Scarlett. It was too soon."

He just felt stalled in their relationship. Stymied.

He'd fallen too fast.

Stupid, he told himself. At some point, he'd convinced himself she was ready for a serious relationship when he'd known she wasn't. Or he'd told himself he could be patient. Date her until she was ready.

But that obviously wasn't going to work either—not if he kept kissing her like he just had. And she'd let him. So did she like him or not?

Like is a long way from love, he thought.

"So, why don't you just tell me what you want?" he asked. "Because I'm getting some mixed signals from you."

"Mixed signals?"

"You clearly, well, I thought it was clearly. I thought you liked me. I mean, I just kissed you like we're practically married." He hooked his thumb over his shoulder, a sliver of fury winding its way through his bloodstream. "I mean, I used to kiss my wife like that before we'd—" He clenched his teeth again, his jaw so tired already.

"But you don't want to spend much time with me, because you suggested going to Disneyland." Hudson wanted to leave. Get out of this situation, away from this beach. He stood up, wondering if there was any rectification for what he'd said.

He started cleaning up from breakfast, putting the bagels back in the bag and the lid on the cream cheese.

Scarlett sat there while he worked, and Hudson hated that he'd said anything at all. He should've just gone to Disneyland. Maybe he shouldn't have kissed her so passionately. He definitely shouldn't have asked her on this trip.

He went into the camper shell and put everything away, taking a moment to look up to where she'd slept the night before. His breath caught in his throat, and he was definitely in love with her.

"I think we should go back to the ranch," she said from behind him, and he spun toward her.

His hopes fell like lead balloons as he crossed to the steps and went down to the asphalt. "All right."

She lifted her chin and looked him square in the eyes. He liked her fire, her determination. "I like you Hudson. That's why I kiss you the way I do."

He nodded, but his ego was taking a beating and his vacation was being cut short. "I more than like you, Scarlett," he whispered.

"But I'm not ready for—you more than like me?" She felt back a step, absolute horror in her eyes.

"Forget it," he said. "Let's go. You want to ride up front with me or in the camper shell?" He wanted to be alone, but he didn't want to ask her to drive an unfamiliar vehicle in bad traffic.

I'm not ready.

She didn't need to say anything else. Didn't need to finish that sentence. Foolishness and fury raced through him. He'd felt like this before too, and it had sent him on the road for thirteen months.

He didn't want to run away this time. Didn't want to leave Last Chance Ranch at all. Could he simply go back to working with Scarlett without kissing her? He wasn't sure.

He wasn't sure of anything anymore.

"I just need more time," she said.

"That's fine, Scarlett." He stepped over to the truck and opened the driver's side door. "Let's go."

They drove back to the ranch in silence, her in the cab with him but clear over on her side of the bench seat. He pulled into her driveway and went around back to get her suitcase out of the shell.

He set it on the sidewalk as she rounded the front of the truck and backed up. "I'm really sorry this didn't work out."

She jerked her attention to him. "This? This trip? Or this...what?"

He gestured between the two of them. "This."

"Are you breaking up with me?"

"I thought you weren't ready." Hudson was so tired, and his brain wasn't working right.

"I'm not ready, but I don't think that means we need to break up."

"Really?" He took a step toward her but immediately rocked back. "I don't think I can do casual." He shook his head. "Not with you."

"Not with me?" she challenged. "What does that mean?"

"I already told you what it meant." He turned and walked away. "I'm going to grab Hound, and we'll be back on Monday."

"You're leaving again?" she called after him.

At the corner of the house, he looked back. Even from a distance, he saw the distress on her face. He didn't want to be the cause of it. But she wasn't ready. He couldn't do casual. It felt like an impasse they couldn't reconcile right now.

"I need a vacation," he said, moving again. He just had to get to Gramps's house and get his dog. Then he could hit the road again. It wasn't even noon yet, and he still had plenty of time to get the rest and relaxation he needed.

Sure, he'd have to do it alone, but he'd spent months and months by himself recently. He could do it again.

He couldn't believe he was lying to himself again, trying to convince himself of something he knew to be false.

But it was better than admitting the truth—that he didn't want to be alone again, not after finding Scarlett. Kissing Scarlett. Falling in love with Scarlett.

"WHERE DO you want me to go?" he asked the empty cab as he drove away from the ranch, Hound in the front seat with him. He'd felt like God had led him to Last Chance Ranch, but Hudson couldn't stay right now. So where did God want him?

He didn't want to go back to the beach, as it now held some bad memories for him. He couldn't stay at the ranch.

He'd been thinking about going to visit his parents, and as the thought came to him again, he wondered if the Lord was leading him in that direction. Problem was, Hudson would almost rather go back and face Scarlett than show up at his parents' doorstep after all this time.

He drove around a bit, the pull west growing stronger and stronger as the day wore on. He stopped for lunch only ten minutes from the ranch, and when he got back in the truck with Hound, he made the inevitable turns that would take him toward the horse boarding stables in the Glendora foothills.

He knew the turns by heart, and he made them almost subconsciously. As he pulled under the familiar archway that said Thousand Oaks, his anxiety skyrocketed. The roads all looked the same. The office building that welcomed people to the stable needed to be repainted, and as he eased past the stables and barns and fields to the homestead way at the back of the property, he noticed how much older everything looked.

Or maybe he was the older one now. Maybe his memory wasn't as sharp as it once had been. Or maybe Hudson couldn't see anything in a positive light now that he didn't have Scarlett to kiss goodnight.

He pushed her from his mind, but she didn't go far. Far enough for him to pull into the driveway and face the house where he'd grown up. "All right, Hound," he said. "This is it."

He didn't get out though. Just sat in the truck and watched the front door until his father came out onto the porch. He wore the same thing Hudson had always seen him wear: jeans and a T-shirt. Cowboy hat. Cowboy boots.

His father leaned against the pillar at the top of the porch and folded his arms. Hudson got out of the truck slowly and waited for his dog to jump down after him. "Hey, Dad," he said as he shuffled up the front walk toward his father.

"Nessa," his dad called over his shoulder. "Your son came to visit." Then he turned and walked back into the house, never looking back.

Chapter Twenty-One

S carlett looked at herself in the mirror, just to be sure all evidence of her afternoon of sobbing had been erased in the shower. And she hadn't spent a colossal amount of money on professional makeup in the city so everyone would be able to see her distress.

She wasn't sure she'd be able to pull anything over on Adele, but she had a new boyfriend so it was possible she'd be distracted enough to believe Scarlett had gotten sunburned and come home early because of it.

They'd been going to church together on Sundays, but since she and Hudson were supposed to be gone tomorrow, perhaps Adele would just let Scarlett sleep. Or cry. Or half-sleep while she cried.

But now, she drew in a deep breath and squared her shoulders. She liked the way this black tank top with the thick straps made her shoulders look smaller, and she wanted to take a yoga class in the hopes she'd find her center. Find what plagued her and pluck it out. Figure out what she needed to do to be ready to take another step with Hudson.

Because it was clear he was ready to take the step. She could hardly believe it, after only a couple of months, but he'd whispered things to her that she couldn't unhear.

Didn't want to unhear.

I already told you what it meant.

She'd been thinking about that sentence from him all day. It ran through her mind while she tried to sing lyrics to her favorite songs to drive the thought away. She'd asked him what it meant that he couldn't "do casual" with her, and he'd said, "I already told you what it meant."

I more than like you.

That was what it meant. He'd meant he was in love with her, and he couldn't just have a casual relationship with her while she figured out if she was ready to fall in love with him.

Pain radiated through her core, but she turned away from her reflection, her ponytail perfectly high on the top of her head. Her makeup was flawless. She'd put on her most flattering workout clothes.

She was ready for a baby goat to jump on her back while she tried to fold her body into complex yoga poses.

Adele had told her the sessions were full, especially on the weekends, but Scarlett wouldn't be turned away on her own ranch. She left the house and crossed the road, glancing at the dairy cows that grazed in the pasture between the homestead and the Goat Grounds.

The lot was filling with cars as she walked along the dirt road, and she caught a glimpse of Carson and his big, black cowboy hat as he checked people into the class. He wore cowboy boots, and jeans, and a T-shirt the color of grape jelly, and Scarlett wondered if Hudson had spoken to him at all.

She wasn't going to act like she was in junior high, and go running to his best friend to find out if he'd said anything about her. Just looking at Carson, though there had never been a spark between them, made her heart pound a little too hard. He was exactly like Hudson—a picture-perfect cowboy with those impossibly wide shoulders and white teeth—and Scarlett just needed a break from cowboys.

She wasn't going to get one. She owned a ranch for crying out loud. So she stepped up to Carson when there was a break in check-ins, and said, "Hey, Carson."

"Scarlett." He smiled at her and glanced down at his clipboard.

"I brought my own mat," she said, indicating the roll on her back. "I'll just find a spot in the corner. I wanted to get a closer look at what you guys do here." She'd never particularly liked yoga, but she couldn't stay home right now either. The goats and Adele were already working the crowd, and she stood in her cute yoga pants, more weight gone from her frame. A flash of jealousy hit Scarlett that her friend seemed to be melting before her very eyes and still cooked delicious food every night.

She fed a baby goat something as she spoke to a couple. They laughed, and Adele's eye caught Scarlett's. Dang. She'd been hoping to set up in the corner unnoticed. She continued in that direction anyway, hoping the real clients and the goats would prevent Adele from coming over to ask her what in the world she was doing there.

Not only in the class, but back on the ranch at all.

Adele took a couple of steps toward Scarlett when Carson called her name. She looked at him, and then back at Scarlett, a clear war raging on her face. Scarlett waved at her to go see what Carson needed, and she opened her mat in a casual gesture.

She sat on the ground, wondering how in the world she was going to do yoga. She wasn't exactly flexible, or thin, and she had a flash of regret before a goat leapt right onto her back. "Oh," she said, surprised as a giggle leaked out of her mouth. Laughing was always better than crying, and as the goat jumped down, she stroked his back, a sense of calmness infusing her soul.

It only stayed for a moment, but it was better than the helplessness that had descended on her that day.

So she stayed for the whole yoga class, though she had to take a breather in the middle of it as a bout of dizziness overcame her from all the bending and deep breathing. Apparently, she hadn't been breathing properly for forty-three years, and her body didn't like the way she was suddenly doing it.

Both Adele and Carson stood at the exit as the patrons exited, long after the cool-down and the picture opportunities. Scarlett had stayed too, though she didn't care about making a human pyramid with a goat topper. Carson had finally put all the goats away before joining Adele and thanking everyone for coming.

With the arena finally empty, Scarlett approached her friends. "What are you guys doing for dinner?"

"Nothing," Adele said quickly, taking a step away from Carson as if they'd both get fired if Scarlett found out they'd been kissing behind the barn. Or wherever that had been happening.

"What are you doing back?" she asked, which drove a wedge right into Scarlett's shivering heart.

"I got sunburned," she said. "My back looks like a lobster." No way she was telling them she'd barely ventured out from beneath the umbrella, and only after she'd changed out of her bathing suit.

"And you came to yoga and let a baby goat jump on your back?" Adele cocked her hip and folded her arms. "You're such a liar."

"Fine," Scarlett said. "Things didn't go well, and Hudson broke up with me. Then he left the ranch." Her chin trembled as she raised it. "I didn't want to be alone, so I came to yoga class." She pushed past both of them, determined not to let her tears fall in front of them.

Going out in public had been a very bad idea. Very bad indeed.

"Scarlett," Adele called after her, but Scarlett didn't stop walking.

Her friend caught up to her easily anyway. "You broke up?"

"I don't know. I really don't want to talk about it."

"Well, too bad. You muscled your way into my place weeks ago and practically demanded I tell you everything."

"Fine." Scarlett stopped in the middle of the road. "I freaked out. Got too far inside my head. Whatever. But the point is, I'm not ready for a man like Hudson."

Adele glared at her. "And what's a man like Hudson like?"

One who loves me. Scarlett thought the words, but she didn't say them. She couldn't. She didn't deserve a man like him—one with money, success, good looks, a strong work ethic, and faith.

She had hardly any of those things, though she did consider herself a fairly hard worker and she believed in God. She seized onto her faith and sent a prayer heavenward that she'd be able to find the confidence and strength everyone around her seemed to already have.

"Scarlett?" Adele asked, but Scarlett just shook her head.

"I just didn't want to be alone tonight. I'll go see what Gramps is doing." She walked away from Adele, who surprisingly let her go. After several long strides, Scarlett looked back and saw her shaking her head at Carson and then looking at Scarlett again.

"I'LL HAVE the double cheeseburger with sweet potato fries," she said, handing the menu back to the server. She looked at Gramps, who was still studying the menu like it was written in Japanese. "You're up, Gramps."

"What's good here?" he asked the waitress, his eyebrows furrowed.

"Gramps, you've been coming here for years," she said. "You like the steak sandwich, remember?"

"I do like a good steak sandwich," he said, still searching the menu.

Scarlett pointed to the menu, on the right near the bottom. "It's right there. Comes with fries or tots."

"I like the fries."

"Steak sandwich and fries," the waitress said.

"Yes." Scarlett picked up Gramps's menu and handed it to the server. "Thanks." She flashed a smile, glad she could still put on a good performance of happiness when she needed to. "So how was your weekend with the dogs, Gramps?"

"Only got 'em for one day," he grumbled. "Hound's gone, and you're home now so Billy and Bob won't stay with me."

"Sure they can," she said, unsure of how she'd sleep in the huge homestead without her dogs with her. Without Hudson on the ranch. Without knowing where he was and if he was coming back.

"Everything on the ranch is looking so good," Gramps said, a smile forming on his face.

"Thanks, Gramps."

"I'm so glad you're here," he said next. "Your grandmother would've been so happy with what you've done." He beamed at her. "And I'll admit I love seeing the ranch thriving too. So many animals, so many people there. It feels right."

"It does feel right, doesn't it?" She took a drink of her soda. "Tell me more about Grams," she said. "She ran the adoption program before?"

"Yes, she was determined to make sure every animal found a good home, whether that was on our ranch or with someone else." He paused to take a breath and then a sip of his water. "Even when she got sick, she went over to that adoption center every day. Even if it was just for an hour."

Scarlett thought about her grandmother, sick with cancer and dealing with chemotherapy treatments, dedicating her healthiest hours to the adoption center on the ranch. Scarlett could get through this hour. And then the next one. And then another. She wasn't sick, and she wasn't going to count the way her heart twisted painfully in her chest. Or how hollow her stomach felt.

Her burger came, and she tried to fill the emptiness in her soul the way she always had—with food.

A WEEK PASSED, and then two, and Hudson didn't show up on the ranch. His name didn't brighten the screen of her phone. He'd texted Carson on the Monday he and Scarlett were originally supposed to return from the relaxing beach vacation to say he'd like a few weeks off. He'd asked Carson to run it by Scarlett, which the cowboy had done.

So in the end, Hudson had resorted to the junior high tactics of talking through a mutual friend. Scarlett had said it was fine for him to take some time off, and she'd begun praying he'd be back in time for his birthday.

She had party plans, and she remembered telling him, *I want you on your birthday.*

And she still did. But July was days away from ending, and his birthday was only four days into August. She only had a week to figure out how to get him back to Last Chance Ranch on the evening of the fourth.

Considering the fact that she hadn't spoken to him in weeks, and that she was still crying in the few minutes before she went to bed, Scarlett wasn't hopeful that she'd be able to see him on his birthday.

Still, she stopped by Adele's the following evening to

ask her if she was still planning to make a birthday cake for Hudson.

"You're still doing the party?" she asked, her eyebrows sky-high. She wore an apron, and she wiped her hands on it. "Come in." She glanced left and right as if the paparazzi had found the ranch and wanted to interview her.

"Yes," Scarlett said as she crossed the threshold into Adele's cabin. She turned and met her best friend's eye. Tears gathered in hers, and Scarlett thought they might just fall. Her voice felt stuck in her throat.

"I have to get him back," she said, her voice breaking as it filled with emotion. A tear splashed her cheek, and she swiped at it without looking away from Adele. "This is different than Vance, Adele."

"Oh, honey." Adele stepped into her and hugged her tight. "Of course this is different than Vance. You're in love with Hudson."

Scarlett shook her head as she cried. "No, not yet. But I think I could fall for him."

"Trust me, you already have."

"Why does he like me?"

Adele pulled away and gave Scarlett a stern look. "Because you're awesome? How about that? You brought this failing ranch to life in what? A month? You work like a dog. You're kind. You're thoughtful. Faithful. Gorgeous. What's not to like?"

Adele walked back over to her hotplate and started stirring before adding a handful of shredded cheese. "You just need to figure out how to love yourself, Scarlett. Then you'll see I'm right, and you're already in love with Hudson."

Figure out how to love herself. Scarlett desperately wanted to do that. She just didn't know how.

Chapter Twenty-Two

Hudson mucked out all fifteen stalls in the green stable, it being a Wednesday. He'd been at Thousand Oaks for three weeks now, and the work was familiar and easy. His mother was thrilled he'd come home to visit, and his dad had put him to good use immediately.

His mom hadn't mentioned a single thing about Jan, and Hudson had settled into a routine that had him eating lunch with his mother and making his own dinner in his own cabin down by the main stables.

That way, he didn't have to see his father very often, nor his brother Jude, who strutted around the place like managing a schedule of cleaning stalls and feeding horses made him more important than everyone else.

Misery had been a constant companion, but he could clean out dirty straw unhappily as well as he could happily. He didn't whistle the way he used to, and his patience with the stubborn horses who didn't want to go out to the exercise ring while he freshened up their stalls sat at low most of the time.

He couldn't believe he'd come back to Thousand Oaks for more than a couple of hours. He hadn't intended to stay, but he didn't have anywhere else to go. He'd texted Carson about having a few weeks off from Last Chance Ranch, and the other cowboy had relayed the message to Scarlett.

She'd given her permission, a seal on the fact that she didn't want to be around him any more than he wanted to pretend that working together would be enough for him. Nothing short of having her to be his wife would be enough for him.

He knew that now, after all this time away from her. Of course, he'd known it on the beach as he'd watched her setting out their breakfast.

His heart pinched in his chest, and yet he was able to keep working. Use the pitchfork to transfer the old straw to the wheelbarrow. Sweep out the corners. Fill the troughs with fresh water. Once all the stalls were done, he put in fresh straw and new sawdust.

Task by task, the work got done. Hudson didn't have to think hard about the work, which meant Scarlett stayed in the front of his mind constantly. The more time that went by, the more foolish he felt.

He was going to be forty-six-years-old next week, and he shouldn't have to communicate through someone else. He also didn't want to have a birthday without Scarlett.

I want you on your birthday.

And yet, she hadn't texted or called him since he'd left the ranch.

"And you don't want her to," he told himself as he went outside to get the horses off the exercise circles. He wanted Scarlett. He loved Scarlett. But he didn't want her in the fragile condition she was in.

He didn't want her to feel badly about herself. He didn't like it when she put herself down, and compared herself to others, and worried constantly that she was good enough for him. He wanted the strong, capable, confidant woman he'd seen pull the ranch back from the brink of collapse. How she could do that and not understand how amazing she was, he didn't know.

He finished in the green stable, a good morning's worth of work done. Back at the house, his mother stood at the stove, stirring something.

"Hey, Mom," he said, the scent of marinara registering in his mind. "Spaghetti today?"

"Yep. How are the greenies today?"

"Fine," he said. He knew his brother and father had given him the stables with the lower-level client's horses. Those that were just here for a couple of nights or that didn't have owners with big houses on the beach or in

Hollywood. Hudson didn't care. He didn't need the money.

He just needed a place to belong.

Desperation choked him, and he pushed it away. He didn't want to belong at Thousand Oaks—and he'd known since he was fifteen years old that he didn't belong here.

He sighed as he sat at the kitchen counter, and his mother looked at him. "What's wrong, Hudson?"

"Nothing, Mom."

She'd been asking him the same question nearly every day since he'd shown up on the front porch. She'd come running out to meet him as his father had walked away. At least he had one person on this planet who wanted to see him and talk to him.

"I know there's something wrong." She put a plate in front of him. "You're not who you used to be."

"Yeah, well, that's true." Hudson reached for a fork and let his mom serve him a mountain of spaghetti. His stomach growled, and he'd eat it all just to make her happy. "People change," he said.

"You're not happy," she said.

"Yeah, well, I'm starting to wonder if I ever will be." He glanced at her, but she was busy twirling the tongs through the noodles and putting them on her plate.

She came around the counter and sat next to him, the way she had been for the past few weeks. They'd talked about his brothers and father, the boarding stables, and the new sewing projects she worked on. Nothing too serious, despite her constant inquiries about what was wrong with him.

What was wrong was that his heart had been shattered.

"I just want to apologize about Jan," his mom said, her voice quiet. "I never should've sided with her, or done anything for her, or...any of it."

"Thank you, Mom," Hudson said, a brief moment of curiosity hitting him. "Did something happen with her?"

"Nothing worth talking about," she said. "But honey, there's something not right with you. More than just Jan. I mean, I don't want to rush your healing, but it seems like your wandering would've cured you of anything with her."

"It did, Mom."

"Then what's wrong?"

He had a feeling she wasn't going to give up today. "I met a woman named Scarlett," he said, taking another big bite of pasta. "This is great, Mom. Thanks for making me lunch every day."

They ate in silence for a few minutes while Hudson wondered what his brother would assign him to do that afternoon. At least Jude spoke to him, even if it was with contempt.

"Your father wants to have dinner tonight," his mom said.

"No, thanks," Hudson said. "I got one of those spinach

mushroom pizzas I like when I went into town a few days ago."

"He wants to apologize," she said.

Hudson sighed, because while he'd taken a break in his church attendance, his prayers and pleas to God hadn't ceased. He simply felt lost, as the Lord hadn't been too keen to direct him after he'd gotten to Thousand Oaks.

"Will Jude be there?" he asked.

"Yes, and Brent is coming from the city."

"Oh, a real family reunion," he said dryly.

"Well, Whip can't get off work, so not quite." She nudged him, and he found a smile on her face when he looked at her. "Please, Hudson. It's time to be done with this."

"*This* has never been my fault," he said, unable to hold the words back.

"I know that," she said. "Brent's bringing ribs and mashed potatoes from Rosco's."

"Oh, now you're just being cruel," he said. "Because pizza doesn't compare to barbecue."

"So you'll come?"

Hudson didn't see how he had a choice. "Fine," he said. "What time?"

"Knock, knock," Brent said as he pushed through the front door of Hudson's cabin. He'd thought the cabin at

Last Chance Ranch had been a huge step up from the camper shell, and it had been. This cabin on his family's boarding stable property sat somewhere in the middle of that, with only a loft that Hudson had to climb into each night to sleep.

"Brent." Hudson left the peanut butter sandwich on the counter and took a few steps over to his brother. "Hey." He hugged his brother and slapped him on the back. "How was the drive?" They stepped back from one another, and Hudson returned to his sandwich.

"Good enough," Brent said. "You can't avoid the traffic."

"Nope." Hudson put the two slices of bread together and took a bite. "You want a sandwich?"

"I thought we were eating dinner with Mom and Dad."

"And Jude," Hudson said. "I don't need any comments about how much I eat, and how much Mom's started spending on lunch since I got back."

Brent smiled and shook his head. "I wish I could argue with you, but." He shrugged and stepped over to the counter. "Why are you back? I distinctly remember you saying you'd *never* come back here."

"I was just going to stay for a couple of days." Hudson took another big bite.

"You met someone." Brent dipped the knife into the peanut butter. "Is that why you've been avoiding my calls?"

Hudson only shrugged, his mouth still full of bread and peanut butter. But yes, he hadn't wanted to talk about the ranch he'd left, and he didn't want to lie either. So, yes, he hadn't answered his brother's Sabbath Day calls.

Hudson had left the boarding stables on Sundays, long before his parents were up so when his mother invited him to church, he could claim he was gone already. Which he was—just not to church.

"What's her name?"

"Who?" Hudson asked, not really willing to have this conversation, even with Brent.

"Come on," Brent said, lifting his sandwich to his mouth.

"Scarlett," Hudson said. "But I don't want to make a big deal about it."

"You don't want to make a big deal about it?" Brent let his sandwich drift to the countertop. "She drove you back home. *Home*, Hudson, where you've hated since you were fifteen years old."

"I just...." Hopelessness filled him, and he shoved the rest of this sandwich in his mouth.

"How long are you planning to stay?"

"Until I can figure out how to face her again."

"Oh, I've got to hear more about this woman," Brent said, taking a bite of his sandwich.

"Later," Hudson said. "We have to be down to the house in ten minutes. Better cram that in your mouth." He reached for his jacket, not because it was cold, but because he could fiddle with the rock he'd taken from the ranch. He'd stopped beside Prime, the robot he'd fixed for Scarlett, and taken a single rock. He wasn't even sure why he'd done it.

But now, as his fingers touched the rock, a sense of peace came over him. A flash of thought came to him that he should text Scarlett. Just something simple. Maybe a hello.

He pulled out his phone and stared at the screen, his heart thumping in his chest in an irregular way. With Brent only a few feet away, Hudson didn't feel like he had the privacy he needed.

It's Hudson. Just thinking about you. Hope things are well at Last Chance Ranch.

Was it revealing too much to say he was thinking about her? Was it too pushy? Did she even care?

He thought about the last kiss they'd shared on the beach, and he had to believe she liked him, missed him, and thought about him too.

"Ready?" Brent asked, half his sandwich still in his hand as he opened the front door of the cabin.

Hudson hit send on the text and said, "Yeah, let's go."

Brent drove down to the house, and though they walked in five minutes before they'd been instructed to show up, they were the last ones there. He heard his mom say, "They're here. Are you ready, Thomas?"

His dad said something, but his voice was too low for Hudson to make sense of the word. His mother appeared around the corner that led into the kitchen, a bright smile on her face. "Brent, you made it." She hugged him first, then Hudson though he'd seen her a few hours ago. "Come in, come in. The food is hot."

"I thought you were bringing the food," Hudson said, looking at Brent.

"I did. I stopped here first." He grinned at Hudson, though he too wore a bit of his nerves in his eyes.

Hudson wasn't quite sure what to expect in the kitchen, but he stepped into the dining room to find the Thanksgiving china on the table. The silverware had been polished and everything. Jude looked up from where he was putting cloth napkins at each seat, and the malice in his eyes was a touch softer than usual.

His father stood at the island where Hudson usually ate lunch with his mother, and he held a pair of tongs as he coated the ribs in barbecue sauce. He looked up as Hudson and Brent walked in, and everything stilled.

"Hey, Dad," Hudson finally forced out of his throat, the same words he'd said to him weeks ago when he'd arrived.

"Hudson." That was an improvement, and Hudson would take it for now. "Brent. This food looks great."

"It should be," Brent said. "Rosco's is the best barbecue in five counties." He moved past Hudson as if his feelings had never been hurt before. Hudson wished he could forgive as easily as Brent, but some of his feelings remained hard.

Watching him interact with their mom and dad so effortlessly brought emotion to the back of Hudson's throat. He glanced at Jude, who was also watching the scene in the kitchen. Hudson didn't want to hover in the dining room so he took a couple of steps toward the food and his family.

Jude stepped in front of him before Hudson had crossed fully into the kitchen. "Look, Hudson, I just want to say that I'm really sorry."

"For what?" Hudson asked before he could censor himself. He wasn't sure if he was supposed to do that tonight or not.

"For treating you badly for so long."

Hudson simply looked into his brother's eyes, trying to erase the years of ridicule Jude had given him for being a mechanic instead of wanting to take over the boarding stable.

"Really," Jude said. "But now that you're back, I could really use your help with things."

"I'm not back for good," he said at the same time Brent said, "He's not staying forever."

"You're not?" Jude glanced to Brent and back. "But you sold your shop in Santa Monica."

"I have a job at a ranch up the road a bit," Hudson said. "I need to get back to it...eventually." He wasn't sure when, so his dad's question was especially hard to answer.

"When?"

"I don't know," Hudson said. "Probably after my birthday."

"Thomas," his mother said. "Don't you have something you want to say before we eat?"

His dad looked like he'd been hit with a baseball bat, and he blinked a couple of times. "Yes, yes, I have something to say." He held a plate in his hand, gripping it tightly with all his fingers.

He swallowed, and Hudson's mother put her hand on her husband's arm. "Go on, Thomas." Her voice held more authority than usual, and she looked at him and then nodded toward Hudson in a not-so-subtle manner.

"It's fine, Mom," Hudson said. "Let's just eat."

"No," she said. "This has gone on long enough, and I'm tired of it. Now, Thomas, talk to your son."

Hudson looked at his dad again, awkwardness filling the kitchen and dining room.

"I'm sorry, son," his dad said. "I've treated you badly for a number of years, and I...apologize. I hope you can find a way to forgive me."

Hudson had been expecting an apology, but now that he'd heard it, he didn't know what to say. He *had* been treated badly for a number of years. His hard feelings softened, melting inside him though they'd taken years to solidify.

"It's okay, Dad."

"No, it's not okay," his dad said. "Don't say it's okay. I

know you won't be able to forgive me right away, but maybe one day." He looked at his wife. "Maybe you won't stay away from the stables for decades now. Your mother would love to have you here more often, and...I wouldn't mind either."

Hudson breathed in and out, and then went around the counter and drew his dad into a hug. "Thanks, Dad." They embraced for a moment, and all of Hudson's feelings felt like mush by the time his dad pulled away.

"Let's pray so we can eat," his mother said. "Brent, will you?"

Brent folded his arms, waited a moment for everyone else to do the same, and he said a blessing on the food.

"All right," his dad said, clearing his throat. "Let's eat." He'd put a few ribs on his plate and moved down to the potatoes so Hudson could load up his plate with his all-time favorite food. He had ribs, potatoes, and salad and had stepped into the dining room when the doorbell rang.

"Was Whip coming?" Jude asked.

"No," his mother said, frowning at the wall that separated the kitchen from the living room and the front door. "I'll get it." She set her partially full plate on the counter and maneuvered between all the men until she ducked out of the dining room.

Hudson put his plate on the table and turned back to get a glass of orange punch. Ready to eat, and finally feeling better than he had in weeks, he paused, his fingers gripping the glass tight, tight, tighter at the sight of the two women standing in the doorway.

"Scarlett?" He didn't remember releasing his cup, but the splash of punch on the floor and the shattering of glass testified that he had.

"Hey, Hudson," she said, lifting her hand and waggling her fingers.

Chapter Twenty-Three

Scarlett swallowed, trying to get her nerves out of her throat so she could speak. Hudson's family was clearly gathered for dinner, and she wished she'd called him before just showing up.

But it had taken so long for her to remember what the name of his family's boarding stable was called, and this was the fourth place she'd visited this week. She hadn't even known it would be the right place. She just knew his stables had the word Oaks in it.

"I guess I found the right boarding stable," she said. "Thousand Oaks. Did you know there's a lot of boarding stables with Oaks in the name? Three Oaks. Forever Oaks. Johnson Oaks." She ticked them off on her fingers, her nerves firing like they were putting out a twenty-one gun salute.

She swallowed and looked around at the other people

in the room. Two of his brothers, obviously. His father. No one moved to clean up the spilled punch or broken glass, and Scarlett said, "I can help."

She grabbed the roll of paper towels off the dining room table, wondering if Hudson would ever say anything to her. She crouched down and had touched the paper towel to the floor before Hudson said, "Scarlett," this time without the question mark at the end. "Stop. You don't need to clean this up." He stepped back and came down to the floor next to her, lightly touching her hand with his fingers.

"Someone does." She looked up, into his brilliant eyes, and time froze. "I'm so sorry," she whispered. "Please come back to the ranch. I'm dying without you." She couldn't believe she'd said that, but it was true.

"And you should see Trixie. She's moping around no matter what Sawyer does for her. And Billy and Bob keep asking about Hound, and." She drew in a shaky breath. "And I miss you. I miss you so much, and—"

She cut off as Hudson pressed his lips to hers. Scarlett thought she'd missed him before, but now that he was kissing her again, she realized she hadn't explored the depth of how much she needed him in her life.

"I'm sorry," she said again, pulling back for a moment. "I love you, and I need you back at the ranch."

"I'll come back," he said, his voice low and full of emotion. Their eyes met again, and this time he wore a smile in his. "Maybe you'd like to meet my family and stay for dinner first?"

Horror struck Scarlett's chest like lightning, and she glanced up at his mom, who stood there with one hand pressed to her heart and the other covering her mouth as she wept.

"No wonder you haven't come to visit until now," she said.

Hudson straightened first, taking Scarlett's hand and helping her to her feet too. "Mom, this is my girlfriend, Scarlett. I think I mentioned her to you."

"Once," she said, looking at Scarlett and now her son. "You should've seen him. He's been nothing but miserable since he showed up here." She drew Scarlett into a hug, and for the first time in a while, Scarlett didn't feel self-conscious that someone was holding her—all of her—tight.

His mother stepped back and said, "This is my husband, Thomas. Hudson's father." The man had stood from his plate at the table and shook her hand.

"Nice to meet you, Scarlett."

"My brothers," Hudson said, putting gentle pressure on her lower back as he turned her toward one of the other men. "Brent." He nodded to the man on his other side. "Jude."

Brent was the brother Hudson stayed in contact with, and Scarlett grinned at him. "I've heard a lot about both of you." She shook their hands, feeling only a sense of family in the house. She'd been expecting awkwardness and discontent, but none of that existed here.

She went right back to Hudson's side, almost wanting to leave so they could talk though the food smelled great.

"Stay and eat with us," his mother said, and Scarlett saved the things she wanted to say to Hudson.

She nodded and Brent took her by the arm and drew her away from Hudson with, "I've heard so much about you too. Tell me, how is that new pig Hudson said he named after me?"

"Your family is so great," Scarlett said as they walked down the back steps. "So great. I mean, my mom would never break out her stupid human tricks at dinner. She'd be mortified." She added a laugh to the sentence, her anxiety returning now that dinner was over and she'd have to really talk to Hudson.

"Yeah," Hudson said. "They're all right."

"I thought you said you didn't get along with them."

"My dad hasn't spoken to me in the three weeks I've been here," he said, taking her hand in his. The warmth spreading through her was exactly like the first time she'd held his hand. The first time he'd kissed her. Everything with him felt like her first time, and she hoped it would be the last first time she'd hold hands with a new man. Her last first kiss with a man.

"But tonight, my mom said he wanted to talk to me, and he and Jude both apologized to me."

"And you've been working and living here." She didn't want to pretend like that hurt, because it did. "Why didn't you just come back to the ranch?"

"Because." He blew out his breath. "I told you, I can't be casual with you. I didn't think I could stand to see you on the ranch and not be able to kiss you, or hold your hand, or anything. What was I supposed to do? Walk by as if I wasn't in love with you?"

Scarlett focused on the ground so she wouldn't fall and so he wouldn't see her emotions. Then she decided she didn't care if he saw. She wanted him to see.

She took a couple of extra steps and moved in front of him. "You're going to come back, right? You didn't just say that, did you?"

"What did you say?" he asked, that playful twinkle in his dark eyes. "You're dying without me?"

Scarlett lifted her chin and pressed against his chest so he'd stop walking. After all, she didn't want to trip and fall backward. "Yes," she said, looking him right in the eyes. "That's what I said. And it's true. Everything I said in there is true."

"Everything?" He closed his eyes and leaned down, his forehead coming to rest against hers. He groaned and traced the tip of his nose down her cheek. "All of it? The part where you said you loved me?"

"Yes," she said, her heart whirring in her chest like a

blender. "All of it, including that." She breathed with him. "And in case you're wondering, you still haven't said that to me."

"I haven't?" He caught the corner of her mouth with his lips but didn't kiss her. "You sure?"

"I think I would remember," she said, though she wasn't exactly sure of anything at the moment. "You said you more than liked me, but that's not the same thing."

"No, it's not." He pressed his lips to her throat, and joy exploded through her whole body. He kissed his way to her mouth, where he kissed her the same way he had on the beach all those weeks ago.

"I love you, Scarlett," he murmured, claiming her lips again. "I love you, I love you, I love you."

———

SCARLETT WOKE IN A STRANGE PLACE, her memory slow as she tried to remember where she was. The roof of the camper shell was only a few feet above her face, and she took a moment to draw in a deep breath of the blankets that smelled like Hudson.

Or maybe that was her hair, her clothes, as she'd laid in his arms until well past dark, talking and kissing until she finally remembered she might be in love but she wasn't married to him.

Instead of making the drive back to Last Chance Ranch, she'd taken his offer of sleeping in the camper shell so they could have breakfast together. Scarlett wanted to do everything together with him, and she swung her legs over the side of the bed and let them dangle before dropping down to the step and then to the floor to get dressed.

A knock sounded on the door before she could open her suitcase, and Hudson called, "Can I come in?"

"It's not locked," she said, facing the door as he opened it and climbed up the couple of steps to join her in the tiny space. "I'm not dressed though. I just woke up."

"Mm." He scanned her from her bedhead hair to her bare feet, his eyes glowing with desire when he looked at her again. "I asked for the day off. Thought maybe you'd like to see the place, maybe go for a horseback ride."

Instant fear gripped her heart. She was much too big to get on a horse. But she just smiled up at him, and said, "If you'll help me get on the horse, I'm game for anything."

"All right, I think I can do that." He grinned down at her, kissed her quickly on the mouth, and said, "So get dressed, and I've got coffee on in the cabin. Or hot water for tea, though I can't promise I have the flavor you want. And I'll show you around." He took a step back, a grin on his face. Scarlett felt flames all the way down in her toes, and she gave him a goofy grin back.

"Well, I'll be right in."

He tipped his hat, somehow turned in the impossibly small space, and left the camper shell, closing the door behind him. Scarlett changed quickly and went inside his cabin, which was cooler than outside and smelled deliciously like coffee and Hudson's cologne. Hound got up and approached her, that wonderful smile on his doggy face.

"Hey, boy," she said, scrubbing him behind the ears.

She'd already been in the tiny, single-room space last night, but her confidence that what she could offer her people took another boost. This cabin was all one room, with the only separate area the bathroom. Hudson climbed a ladder and slept in a loft at night, and he said he wouldn't miss that.

"Coffee?" he asked as she poured herself a cup.

"Yeah, I'm feeling like a lot of cream and sugar this morning."

"Oh? Didn't sleep well?"

"I've had a stressful few weeks." She flashed him a look. "I still need to find an accountant, and I've got a couple of people coming next week."

"That's good news."

"And now that you'll be back, I'm really going to have to pull together a party on short notice."

"You don't need to have a party for me," he said.

"Of course I do." Scarlett mixed in a healthy amount of cream and three spoonfuls of sugar. "You only turn forty-six once."

"Forty-six is nothing special."

"You've survived another year," she said. "And at your age, that's something." She turned and looked at him, glad the atmosphere between them was back to flirty and fun.

"Ha ha," he said, setting his cup in the sink. "You wanna take that to go?"

"Sure." Scarlett took a sip of her coffee and followed him out the front door. Hound didn't make a move to come, so she closed the door and left him inside the cabin. "So I've been working mostly in the blue stables and the green stables."

"What do you do?"

"Clean the stalls, work with the horses, feed them, all of that." He walked slowly down a dirt path, seemingly in no hurry. "Now, don't tell Trixie, but I've taken a shine to a horse out here. Her name's Moonbeam, and she belongs to a young couple who just got married and live in an apartment. So Moonbeam's here with us."

"Ooh, Trixie is going to smell this Moonbeam on you so fast." Scarlett laughed, glad when Hudson joined in with her.

He showed her the stables, explained why his great-great-grandfather painted them different colors and how the operation worked.

She drank her coffee and listened to the pride in his voice as he spoke about the boarding stables. "You sure you don't want to be here?" she asked.

"Definitely sure," he said. "I'm hoping you'll let me marry you and move into the homestead with you." He ducked his head when he spoke. "I don't mind waiting however long it'll take you to have the wedding of your dreams, as long as I can kiss you at night and we can talk about serious things."

"I'm okay with that," Scarlett said, committing to it on the spot. "Really, Hudson, I just...it's hard for me to believe that you love me." She choked out the last two words. "Vance, he, well, I haven't been loved in a long time. Sometimes I don't think it's possible for anyone to feel that way about me."

"I know," he said. "I mean, I think I have some idea of what it feels like to wonder what is so wrong with me that Jan couldn't love me." He squeezed her hand. "So, let's just reassure each other when we need to, all right?"

"I can do that," Scarlett said.

"What made you believe that I liked you?" he asked.

"What do you mean?"

"I mean, you went to Three Oaks, then Johnson Oaks, and then here, not even knowing that I'd be at any of them. Why'd you do that?"

Scarlett let her now-empty coffee mug hang at her side as they walked. "I wanted you to come back to the ranch." She tucked her arm into his. "I got your text about ten minutes before I pulled up, and I sat in my car and prayed and prayed that this place would be the right one. Then I took a deep breath and went to knock on the door. And then there you were." She wanted to be honest with him in all things.

"I'll admit I was kind of a mess," she said. "Adele tried

to get me to call you a bunch of times. I didn't go to church, because I couldn't go by myself."

Hudson tipped his head back and looked up into the trees. "I understand, Scarlett. I felt like God had led me to Last Chance Ranch and then abandoned me. I didn't understand, well, a lot of things actually. But then you showed up, and everything made sense in my life."

Scarlett caught sight of his cabin in the distance, and she sensed this tour was almost over.

Hudson's step slowed. "Scarlett, I wanted to talk to you about something." He sounded serious, and Scarlett's heart skipped a beat.

"Okay," she said.

"It's about having a family," he said, his eyes focused on the horizon.

"Oh." Humiliation filled Scarlett. "Well, I'm past being able to have children, Hudson."

"I'm aware," he said. "Though I think women have babies at age forty-three, but what I was thinking about was actually adoption." He paused and turned toward her. "I know I'm the old man here, but I've always wanted a family."

The weight of his gaze on her drew Scarlett's eyes to his. "I wouldn't mind adopting," she said, the thought rotating around inside her head as it tried to find a place to take root.

"No? Have you thought about it before now?"

"No," she admitted.

"So maybe something to think about," he said, stepping slowly and capturing her hand in his.

"Yeah, I'll think about it," she said.

"How long do you think it will take you to plan a wedding?" he asked next, his voice full of false casualness.

Scarlett shook her head and laughed. "Let's get through your birthday party first, okay?"

He agreed with a chuckle, but Scarlett's mind started down a path she'd forbidden it to go down previously.

The wedding of her dreams. What would that look like, exactly?

In a past life, when she was a different Scarlett, it would've been a huge affair, with the best of everything. But she'd already had that wedding.

And what she wanted this time was simplicity. Her family. Hudson's. Good food made by Adele. A pastor in a small church at the bottom of the bluff.

And her and Hudson, dancing in their finest clothes. She could definitely plan something like that by springtime. Oh, yes, she'd be married in the spring.

The thought didn't hold any fear, and she sighed as she gripped Hudson's hand with both of hers and they went back to his cabin to pack up his stuff so he could come back to Last Chance Ranch with her.

Chapter Twenty-Four

Hudson woke as he usually did on August fourth, but he knew instinctively that something was amiss. "Hound?" He lifted his head off the pillow and looked for his dog, who never slept more than a foot away from Hudson.

Until this morning.

Something was definitely wrong.

Hudson's first thought was that his dog—an eleven-year-old golden retriever—had finally crawled away in the night and passed away. His heart started pounding like a bass drum, and he hurried to get his old bones out of bed.

"Hound?" he called louder, praying that if the dog had died that it had happened peacefully while the canine slept.

The clicking of claws came down the hall as Hudson pulled a T-shirt over his head. "Hey, bud," he said, his adrenaline still soaring through his bloodstream. "There you are. Did I sleep too late? Need to go out?" He scrubbed the dog behind his hears and under his jowls. "Let's go get breakfast, okay?"

He stepped into the hall, a new smell meeting his nose. Bacon.

Someone was in his house, and his heart rate picked up again, hoping for the curvy auburn-haired woman he was in love with.

Sure enough, Scarlett stood in the kitchen, sliding a fried egg out of the pan and onto a plate. Hudson leaned against the wall, a grin on his face. "Well, aren't you the prettiest thing I've ever seen?"

She grinned at him and danced over to nestle herself into his arms. "Happy birthday."

"It's certainly starting out that way." He leaned down and kissed her, tasting cream and sugar and coffee.

"Bacon and eggs," she said, stepping back. "And you're really something, luring Hound away from the bacon. He's been guarding me since I pulled it out."

"Well, he loves bacon." Hudson pinched off a piece and gave it to his dog.

"He loves you more," Scarlett said, looking up at him through her lashes as she picked up a couple of slices of bacon. "Obviously. You called once, and he went on down the hall."

"We've been through some things together," Hudson said, smiling at her. "Thanks, sweetheart. This is great."

He sprinkled salt and pepper on his eggs and enjoyed breakfast with his girlfriend.

"I've been thinking," Scarlett said, and Hudson looked at her.

"Yeah?"

"I have always wanted a family," she said. "It was really hard for me the older I got and I never got pregnant." She looked at him with raw emotion in her expression. "So I'd really like to adopt or foster or whatever with you. We could build a decent family, don't you think?"

"I know we could build a *good* family," he said.

"We have the dogs already," she said. "But I think we could add a baby or two."

Hudson smiled at his almost-empty plate, his emotions swirling up and down. Joy radiated through him, and he felt like the luckiest man in the world when he looked at Scarlett again.

"Have you thought about what else I asked?"

"Oh, you mean the part where you want me to wear a diamond. That part?" she asked, her tone playful and light.

"Yeah, that part," he said. "We could go down to town today. Get a ring. Now *that* would be the best birthday present on the planet."

"You're impossible." She shook her head as she giggled and scooped up another bite of eggs. She pointed her fork at him. "And so manipulative. Using your birthday to get me to go to the jewelry store?"

He grinned at her. "Fine. I'll go myself. I asked for the day off, and my boss gave it to me." He'd proposed to her twice now over the past week but she still hadn't said yes. She'd claimed she wanted to go to the jewelry store with him, pick out her ring, and then she'd become his fiancée.

So him going alone wouldn't fly with her, and he knew it. Still, he leaned away from the counter and folded his arms, watching her.

"You don't need to go yourself," she said, her eyes glittering with a secret. Hudson knew that look, and he leaned forward.

"What have you done?" he asked, half hopeful and half afraid of the answer.

"So I happen to have gone to town a couple of times this week. I may have stopped by the jeweler myself."

Hudson blinked at her, sure he'd heard her wrong. "You did not."

Scarlett left her uneaten food on the counter and moved down a few feet, where she opened a drawer and took out a ring box. Hudson gaped at it, his blood feeling like ice in his veins.

"Scarlett," he said in a dangerous voice. "What is that?"

"I would like to be married in the spring," she said. "Gramps showed me a few pictures of this ranch when all the trees are in bloom, and it's gorgeous. That's eight months from now. I think I can wait that long to be your wife."

She swallowed, the first sign she'd shown him that she was nervous. His anxiety blipped, and his eyes dropped to the ring box again. "Eight months. That's a mighty long time, Scarlett."

"I know," she said. "But it's the wedding I want."

He thought about what he wanted, and that was to wake up next to Scarlett or find her in this kitchen every morning. But he could wait—because ultimately, his greatest desire was for her to be happy. And they wouldn't be living in this cabin anyway.

The cracking of the ring box brought his attention back to her, and he expected to see the ring she wanted sitting there.

Instead, he saw a men's wedding band, and she said, "Hudson Flannigan, I'm hopelessly in love with you. Will you marry me?"

Hudson blinked. Had she seriously just asked him to marry her?

"Don't be mad," she said, pulling the ring out of the box. "I know you don't wear this during the engagement, but I wanted to ask you."

Their eyes met, and all of Hudson's frustration drained away. "This is what our life is going to be like, isn't it?" He grinned at her. "You taking charge."

"I mean, maybe." She shrugged as she set the ring back in the box. "But I like it plenty when you take charge."

Hudson got up and gathered her into his arms. "So if I say yes, can we go to town today and get you a ring?"

"Oh, that's not necessary," she said, opening another drawer.

"How long have these been in my house?" he asked as she pulled out another ring box.

"Just a couple of days." She handed him the box. "This is what you bought for me."

"Oh, I did, huh?"

"I may have taken your card out of your wallet."

"You did what?" Hudson stared at her, trying to decide if he was just shocked, or if he was upset, or if he couldn't wait to get this ring on her finger and call her his fiancée.

"Well, I couldn't buy my own diamond ring," she said, pushing against his chest playfully. "And you just leave your wallet lying around the cabin. Hound was here, and he said I could."

Hudson started shaking his head, laughter bubbling up from deep inside him. "All right, then. I suppose you want to wear this today."

"Yes, please." She looked from him to the box and back. "But you still haven't said yes."

"It's a yes from me, Scarlett," he said, opening the box and finding a beautiful diamond ring inside. He didn't know anything about cuts or shapes, but if she liked it, so did he. "It'll always be a yes from me."

Hours later, with the diamond on her finger and after plenty of kissing, they walked with Hound down the road from his cabin.

"Are you sure we can't cancel the party?" he asked.

"I'm sure."

"I'm just not great at being in the spotlight," he said.

Scarlett cocked her head and said, "Well, too bad. It's one day a year, and it's happening."

He went with her, surprised when they bypassed the homestead. "Where are we going?"

"The horse barn," she said. "Everything's set up in there."

As they approached, he could hear music and chatter, and his hand tightened in Scarlett's. She gave him a reassuring smile and pushed open the doors to reveal a huge banner that said, *Happy Birthday Hudson* on it.

"He's here," she called, and a cheer went up from everyone inside. He spied his parents and his brothers—all three of them—all the ranch hands and a half dozen volunteers. Gramps stood right by the door, a wide smile on his face, and Hudson leaned down and hugged him first.

"Welcome to the family," Gramps said.

"Happy to be here," Hudson said, and it was the absolute truth. As he smiled and shook hands, gave hugs, and loaded his plate with smoked brisket and baked beans, he didn't forget to send a prayer of gratitude to God for leading him to Last Chance Ranch.

Eight months later

S carlett turned and looked at the back of the dress in the mirror. "I think it's okay." She met Adele's eyes. "What do you think?"

"It's the best we can do," she said. "There's no time to run down and get a new button, and no one will be able to tell."

Scarlett had lost another fifteen pounds over the course of the last eight months, but she'd still popped a button on her wedding dress. She pushed the negative thoughts out of her head. Hudson didn't care what she wore to marry him. All he wanted was for her to show up, say I do, and sail off into the sunset with him.

Literally. He'd literally rented a boat—a yacht, really—for a month and they were going to take their own private cruise down to Mazatlán and back. He was paying a staff of three to cook, clean, and drive the yacht, so they could simply relax and spend time together.

No dogs. No horses. No robot mailboxes. That was what he'd said, always followed by, "We work hard, Scarlett. You work so hard. Let me take you on vacation."

And because she did work hard, she'd said yes. She'd even bought four new swimming suits, and she wasn't going to be afraid to wear them in front of him.

Someone knocked on the door, and Scarlett spun away from the mirror. Her mother came in and scanned the dress. "It's beautiful." She hugged Scarlett and added, "Everyone's ready."

"Gramps?"

"He's standing right outside, every seam pressed."

"Thanks, Mom." Scarlett took a deep breath of her mother's perfume, a scent so familiar it made her throat close.

"No crying now," her mom said. "I've seen Hudson, and he's so happy he's glowing."

Scarlett stepped back and smoothed her hands down her stomach. They'd spent more time with his family over the eight months of their engagement than hers, but this certainly wasn't the first time her parents had met Hudson.

"All right, I'm ready."

She left her bedroom and the homestead and headed across the lawn toward Horse Heaven and LlamaLand.

Along the south side of the fields there sat a long row of cherry trees, and they'd bloomed last week into bright pink blossoms.

A tent had been set up at the end of the row, and Scarlett would walk down the aisle created by the trees to get to Hudson.

Gramps waited at the fence, holding onto it with one hand. "Here she is, Dad." Her mother leaned over and pressed a kiss to her father's forehead and said, "Just give me a minute."

She and Adele bustled down to the tent, which was only about a hundred feet away. The world spun, and Scarlett thought, *Please don't let me fall. Or faint. Or trip.*

A sense of peace filled her, and she knew God was with her.

"Your grandmother would've loved this," Gramps said, his voice tight and teary. "We got married on this ranch, you know."

"I know, Gramps." Scarlett squeezed his arm tight against her. "You showed me the pictures. It's why I chose April to get married."

"We were married in April."

"I know, Gramps." Scarlett's worry for her grandfather hadn't diminished over the months. He hadn't called her the wrong name or acted like he was losing his mind. But she was a worrier. That was what she did, especially over those she loved most.

Her thoughts drifted to Adele, who'd left the ranch months earlier to pursue her dreams of becoming a chef. She'd come back for the wedding, but Scarlett didn't think she seemed particularly pleased about being here. She claimed to be happy in New York City, but Scarlett wasn't so sure about that either.

"It's time," she said when she heard the music change down in the tent. She could worry about Adele later. Gramps too. Right now, she was going to get married.

Step by step, she made it down the aisle and under the tent to Hudson. He also kissed Gramps on the top of the head before taking Scarlett's arm in his. They faced the minister together, and everything that was said and done blurred together for Scarlett.

She tried to hold onto each moment. When Pastor Williams said this was a new life for them. When Hudson read his vows to put her happiness above his and to love and cherish her forever. When she said she'd honor and love him until the day she died.

When she said, "I do," and then he echoed it back to her.

When they kissed for the first time as husband and wife. She really held onto that moment, pressing her forehead against his, her fingers tightly bunched in his collar. The cheers and whoops around her didn't deter her from saying, "Our last first kiss."

"What do you mean?" he whispered, obviously just as unconcerned as she was about the crowd watching them.

"I mean, that was our last first kiss. All the others will just be second or third kisses."

He smiled at her and said, "I love you, sweetheart." He turned to the cheering crowd and lifted their joined hands. They swooped back down the aisle, past the pink-blossomed trees, and into the barn.

"So this is where you want to dance?" He looked around, and every detail had been made exactly how she'd dreamt it.

Lanterns hung in the loft, and soft, white Christmas lights filled the huge space. The floor had been swept clean, and several long tables held refreshments near the back wall. Behind them, people started to filter into the barn as they arrived from the ceremony.

"Yes," she said as her dad stepped over to the sound system he'd personally set up. "Now, dance with me, cowboy."

Hudson complied, taking her easily into his arms, and the dream Scarlett had had on the beach all those months ago became a reality. They were wearing their best clothes, surrounded by loved ones, and when Hudson leaned down to kiss her, he wore a soft, love-filled expression on his face.

Scarlett said, "I love you," just before he kissed her, happiness filling her that she'd found this handsome, hardworking, honest cowboy to give her one last chance at true love.

Read on for a sneak peek at **LAST CHANCE COWBOY**, and find out what's going on with Carson and Adele...

Sneak Peek! Last Chance Cowboy - Chapter 1

A dele Woodruff slid her hands down the front of the jeans she'd put on in the dressing room, wondering why she hadn't gotten a more physical job sooner. After all, working twelve hours a day on her best friend's ranch had proven to be the best weight loss solution she'd ever found.

She was down fifteen pounds now, and these jeans showed curves she'd forgotten she had. She turned and looked at her behind in the mirror, deciding these were definitely the jeans she needed. Adele was currently counting pennies to make sure she had the money necessary to pay her bills, but these jeans had practically been made for her body.

So she'd get two pairs. That was reasonable. She worked on a ranch now, for crying out loud, and while she'd only been there a few weeks, her clothes had taken a serious toll. The jeans she'd brought with her were ratty and perpetually dirty, so getting a couple of new pairs wasn't unreasonable.

If only her debt collectors understood what was reasonable and what wasn't. If only Hank, her no-good, used-to-be-stinking-rich ex hadn't put all of his expenses in her name and then skipped town. As one woman at a credit card company had told her several months ago, she didn't care who'd racked up the debt. The fact was, the account was in Adele's name, and the payment was due on the fifth of each month.

Each and every month.

She'd disputed a couple of the bigger cards and found some relief that way, but they'd only offered her a lower payoff amount, with a more aggressive payback schedule.

She pushed the thoughts of Hank and his monumental debt from her mind. She needed jeans and boots to work on the ranch, period.

Oooh, boots, she thought, and detoured over to the shoe department. So the two pairs of boots she bought weren't exactly what one might need to work with goats on a rescue ranch—or what Scarlett, the owner of Last Chance Ranch, hoped would become a rescue ranch. But Adele needed the ankle boots nonetheless.

With her purchases in the back of her car, she stuck the key in the ignition and sent up a prayer. "Come on," she whispered. "Please let it start quickly." She used to pray that she could get the sedan to start on the first try.

But she couldn't remember the last time that had happened, so her pleas to the Lord had changed into *just let it start before I melt in here.*

Sometimes that worked, and sometimes she had to get out of the car and take a break to breathe before trying again. Today, in the mall parking lot, God answered her prayers, because the car started on the third try.

"Thank you," she said, slapping the steering wheel. "This might actually be a new record." She flipped the car into gear and started toward the grocery store. She had dozens of ideas for her food videos, but she was on a very strict budget for them. Yes, her Instagram channel was fairly new, with only about a hundred and fifty videos. She posted a new one each morning, and that meant a lot of cooking in the evening. It meant shopping several times a week. It meant spending money she *almost* had.

But her popularity had been growing lately, especially as she focused more on feeding a ranch crowd than doing what some of the other foodie video channels did— anything and everything.

No, Adele wanted to be niched down, because the audiences there were hungry and loyal. The potential to stand out skyrocketed, and she hadn't seen anyone else doing Beef's Greatest Hits or Budget Meals for Two.

She'd done both of those, but now that she was on the ranch, she wanted to focus on a more country-style approach to cooking. Things that had to simmer and stew, like chicken pot pie or beef tips and gravy. She wanted to do cowboy pizzas, and rustic desserts, and down-home cooking anyone could do.

Anyone with a single hotplate, the most expensive lights in Hollywood, and four video cameras, that was. She'd found all of the equipment from one of Hank's storage units several months back. After all, her name was on the lease, and she was the one they'd contacted when he'd stopped paying the bill. Her choice was to lose everything in the storage unit to an auction or come clean it out.

She'd gone and cleaned it out, finding several treasures —the lights and cameras had sparked her idea to start her own food videos, and she'd sold everything else to pay off one of Hank's cards.

Her channel made a little bit of money now, and she'd vowed to use only that income to buy the groceries she needed for the videos. She was putting a hundred percent of her earnings back into this business, but it was small and fledgling, and she believed in it.

She selected the cuts of meat she needed, then the vegetables, always planning and double-planning her menu to use a lot of the same items so nothing went to waste. She had a good stock of staples—flour, sugar, salt, garlic powder and other spices—by now, and most of her expenses went to the protein she was cooking, or the dairy aisle. Because wow, she'd never really paid attention to how expensive heavy cream was.

She knew now.

She checked out, her bill coming twenty dollars over

what she'd made the previous week. *It's okay*, she told herself. She'd make that twenty dollars back this week with her amazing apple turnover video and the watermelon gazpacho she had planned.

With the food in the backseat next to the boots and jeans, she got behind the wheel again, once again praying for a miracle.

She twisted the key. Nothing happened. Again and again, she tried and the engine just clicked. "Come on," she said, a hint of desperation in her voice. She wiped the back of her hand along her forehead and ignored the people walking by as they headed into the store.

Next time, she told herself as she tried again. And again. She started saying it out loud, but when she'd been trying to get her stupid car started for fifteen minutes, she left the key in the ignition and got out.

Frustration boiled within her. Why couldn't Hank have had a new Mercedes in the storage unit? She could've used that. Guilt immediately cascaded through her. She knew God had blessed her with the lights and filming equipment, and she'd spent hours on her knees thanking Him. So she couldn't be upset about what she didn't have.

And yet, she was.

She paced away from the car, the air hot in the parking lot. At least there was a breeze. The car had working air conditioning, if she could just get it started, but the windows didn't roll down. So she really couldn't sit in it for very long, trying to get the blasted engine going.

If she didn't get back up to the ranch soon, Scarlett would wonder where she'd gone. And Adele didn't want to explain anything, even to her best friend. No one knew about the foodie videos, and she wasn't ready to tell anyone yet.

She returned to the car, actually somewhat disappointed that no one had stolen it while she'd taken her walk around the parking lot. "They probably tried," she muttered. "And couldn't get it started."

She sighed as she got behind the wheel again. Yes, she'd lost some weight, but she had a lot more than fifteen pounds to lose to be considered anywhere close to thin. She left the door open and turned the key again. Counting in her head, she made it to ten, then twenty. She coached herself to get to thirty, then forty, then fifty before she gave up, got out, and kicked the tires.

She didn't make it to fifty, because the engine turned over on try number forty-six.

"Hallelujah," she said, reaching to pull the door shut. She really needed to get Scarlett's new cowboy-slash-mechanic to look at her car. But Hudson Flannigan had been so busy with projects around the ranch, and Adele didn't know him well enough to ask.

Besides, she couldn't pay him. That had kept her mouth shut too.

She flipped the car in reverse and slammed her foot on the gas pedal at the same time she checked behind her. Her car moved, and it seemed to be going at the speed of sound, especially when she saw the huge, white truck behind her.

A horn sounded. She slammed on her brakes. The sedan jerked to a stop. Or had she hit that truck?

Her heart beat in the back of her throat as she put the car in park and opened her door.

"What are you doing?" a man demanded, coming around the front of the truck to see if she'd hit him. She was wondering the same thing, but his condescending tone lit a fire inside her chest.

Or maybe that was this man's rugged good looks. His long legs and broad shoulders. That delicious cowboy hat he wore, revealing only the hint of sandy blond hair, neatly trimmed. His beard was cut close too, revealing a strong jaw Adele could grip while she kissed him.

She shook herself. Kissed him? What in the world was that? Adele was not interested in this pretty-boy cowboy, though her pulse testified that oh, yes she was.

The cowboy hat and boots were obviously for show, because his jeans looked like the ones she'd just purchased. Brand new. Not a speck of dust anywhere. The boots too, looked like he'd never stepped foot on a ranch, a boarding stable, or even dirt.

He wore a shirt in a lighter tint than summer grass, and he clearly had more money than he knew what to do with. When he looked at her, she forgot where she was and why she was so sweaty.

Sweaty. Oh, man, she was *so sweaty* from her fight with starting the car. Why couldn't she meet handsome men while she was dressed in a flirty skirt and with her makeup done just right?

Embarrassment crept through her, but she lifted her chin. This guy was no different than Hank. Sure, he had a black cowboy hat and a pair of boots Hank wouldn't be caught dead wearing, but other than that, he was exactly like her dirty, rotten ex-husband.

"I didn't hit your precious truck," she said.

"Came real close," he said.

"Yeah, well, real close and contact are two different things." She turned and started back toward her seat. He grabbed her arm, and dang, if that didn't send fireworks and a raging inferno of fury through her bloodstream.

She glared at his hand and then up into his eyes. "Get your hands off me. And move your truck. You're causing a traffic jam."

The cowboy removed his hand from her arm as if he'd been burned. He had the decency to look cowed by her. Embarrassed even, hopefully that he'd touched her without her permission.

"What's your name?" he asked.

"You don't need it," she said, getting behind the wheel and closing her door. At least the car was still running, the air conditioner blowing.

She looked in her rear-view mirror to see the big truck still blocking her and that delicious man still staring at her.

It was easier to glare than to smile, and besides, Adele was *not* interested in another billionaire boyfriend. Oh, no, she was not.

Sneak Peek! Last Chance Cowboy - Chapter 2

Carson Chatworth didn't want to get in his truck and leave without getting that pretty woman's name. But she wasn't budging from behind the wheel of her car, and he really was causing a traffic flow problem in the parking lot.

He decided he didn't care. He'd been in California for approximately seventy-two hours and the traffic here was the worst he'd ever seen. Of course, anything was going to be worse than Gold Valley, Montana, where he'd been born and raised. With a population of only fifteen thousand, the traffic could never be that bad.

He glanced around the grocery store parking lot, thinking there were probably fifteen thousand people here right now, trying to get something to eat.

Taking a deep breath, he strode over to her window and knocked on it. She shook her head like mad, her short blonde hair flying around that beautiful face. "I just want to ask you something," he said.

"My windows don't roll down," she said, and he could barely hear her through the glass.

"I don't believe that."

"Believe what you want." She didn't try to roll them down, which meant she'd lied to him. Had he really been that rude? She'd almost smashed into his truck, and that, plus his dogs, was all he had left from his almost forty years in Montana.

"Fine," he practically yelled, frustrated at her and hungrier than he'd been in a while. "I have ways of finding out who you are."

That got her to get out of the car, and she almost hit him with the door as it came flying open violently. "Are you threatening me?" she asked, her blue eyes blazing with fire. "I didn't hit you. Go away."

"I just want to know your name."

"Well, too bad. I have no business with you."

"I'll find out." Why he cared, he wasn't sure. Maybe because she was the first person to make him feel alive since the sale of the ranch. And if he were being honest with himself, long before that even.

"What are you going to do?"

"I got your license plate number. I'll make a few phone calls." He had money, and while he'd never had to throw it around to get what he wanted, he could learn. Oh, yes, if there was one thing Carson Chatworth was doing these days, it was learning all kinds of things he'd never thought he'd have to.

He rounded the front of his truck, catching her muttering, "I hate men like you." He paused, wanting to go back and explain that he really wasn't a bad guy. That she stirred something in him, and he simply wanted a way to contact her later. Maybe take her to dinner so they could get to know each other better.

Their eyes met, and something super-charged flowed between them. For him, it was attraction, but for her, he suspected it was being classified as something else entirely. Probably anger.

That pink tint in her cheeks was so sexy, as was that brilliant, blue tank top and the cute little straw hat she wore. Everything about her appealed to him—well, except the glare. He could do without that.

He tipped his hat at her, glanced at her license plate again, and got behind the wheel of his truck. Once he was out of the way, he reached over to the glove box and got out a slip of paper to write down the letters and numbers before he forgot them.

Then he left this grocery store completely. There would be another one not too far away, and Carson needed space to think.

What he really needed was someplace to call home, as he'd been on the road for over two months. Living in hotels and campgrounds was not the life for him, and he'd applied for a couple of jobs in the area, at local ranches and boarding stables. Surely his lifelong ranching skills could get him on somewhere, preferably Last Chance Ranch, which had advertised a cabin to live in as part of the wages.

He got a sandwich and just drove, having nowhere to go until his interview tomorrow. So he'd drive until he got tired of the vibrations of the road beneath him, and then he'd find a hotel.

With something substantial in his stomach, he reflected on the scene in the parking lot. He hadn't sworn at that blonde woman, or really said anything too bad at all. She'd almost rammed into him, and he was merely checking his vehicle. She'd got out to check too.

Feeling okay with his actions, he rolled down his window and let the warm air blow in. His cowboy hat threatened to get blown away, so he took it off. He cast it a glare, like it was responsible for his father's drinking habit and his brother's online poker addiction.

The debts they'd racked up over the years would've taken Carson his entire life to pay back, and he supposed he should be thankful that the Lord had provided him a way to get out from under their actions. Get away from them.

And he *was* grateful for that. But he was also angry and heartbroken that he'd had to sell Cobble Creek Ranch to do it. He'd only known a Montana summer in all of his thirty-eight years of life, and packing everything he owned into the back of this truck and crossing state lines had cost him more than he'd imagined it would.

But Terry hadn't called once since Carson had left, and he supposed he should put that in the blessings column too. If he were counting those at the moment, which he wasn't.

His father hadn't tried to reach him either, and Carson hoped the two of them were still alive. He didn't hate his father and his brother; he just didn't want to be saddled with taking care of his father's failing health when he did nothing to follow the doctor's directions. Nor did he want to watch Terry play games online when he could be working to bring home the money they needed.

"Disabled," fell from his lips, along with a scoff. Terry was not disabled. He just didn't like working.

"Not your problem anymore," Carson said, and he was at least right about that. But the loneliness he'd experienced since leaving behind everything and everyone he'd ever known had hit him hard. Maybe that was why the woman in the parking lot had lit such a reaction in him.

Tired of driving already, he pulled off the highway and used his phone to find a hotel. Calls, texts, and mapping were about all he used his device for, but it was the best one money could buy.

He'd managed to get the family lawyer on his side and together, they'd split the money from the sale of the ranch so that Carson got fifty-one percent, with the other forty-nine being split between Terry and their father.

Didn't matter. Carson had become a billionaire overnight, and while the number was less in Terry's bank account, there were still nine zeroes at the end. Well, there had been when Carson had left the state of Montana. Who knew what his brother had spent in the past ten weeks.

Another problem Carson didn't have to deal with anymore. His money was safe, protected where neither his father nor his brother could ever access it. He'd bought a new truck, and a new hat, and packed Ted and Tony into the back before driving away.

"Time to stop driving away," he told himself as he went inside to see if this hotel would let him have dogs. The dog waste bags on a pole in the middle of the front lawn was encouraging, and sure enough, they gave him a room for the night no problem.

Now he just had to survive another lonely night before his interview. Yes, his two black labs were great company, but they didn't speak English. They couldn't give advice. He did steal comfort from their loyalty and devotion to him, but what he really wanted was a friend.

He wanted to know who that blonde woman was, and how he might be able to see her again. Because if she would just listen to him, he could explain that he hadn't meant anything by asking her if she'd hit his truck. If they could just talk, then maybe he could ask her out. Maybe he wouldn't have to be alone forever.

THE NEXT DAY, he skipped his morning prayers like he'd been doing for months. God had never seemed to hear him in Montana while he pleaded for a solution to their financial problems that would allow him to keep the ranch he'd grown up working. No, every solution required the sale of their generational land, their herd, crops, all of it.

Not wanting to dwell on the negative, he didn't kneel down as soon as he rolled out of bed. And he'd been happier—at least he thought he was. He worked now, thought things through, and went with what his gut told him. He used to think that was God, leading and guiding his life, but now he wasn't so sure.

Maybe God had abandoned him the way his mother had, all those years ago. She'd been the one to teach him how to fold his arms, how to say a prayer, how to look on the sunny side of life. But apparently, even she had a limit, and she'd left his dad and Cobble Creek Ranch when Carson was only twelve years old.

"Two interviews today, guys," he told Ted and Tony, brothers from a litter he'd bred on the ranch. "Let's hope we get one of them, okay? Then we can find a real house to live in." He straightened his hat and grabbed his duffel bag before heading out to the truck with the dogs.

Last Chance Ranch sat a few minutes up a canyon, the ranch on a bluff that overlooked the valley and bordered the Angeles National Forest. It was beautiful land, and he passed a couple of parked cars for sale at the intersection where he turned to go up to the ranch.

A few minutes later, he arrived at the front gate to the ranch, which was being guarded by a legless robot. It looked like it might be a mailbox, but it was in serious need of repair. He eased his truck by it, noticing instantly that this place was in the process of getting cleaned up.

And whoever was doing it, was doing a great job. *And they need help*, he thought as he passed a couple of roads on his left and nothing but farmland on his right. His heart took courage at the familiar sight of a ranch, and he liked the aura of this place immediately.

He pulled into the driveway of the homestead, as a woman named Scarlett Adams had instructed him, and he said to the dogs, "Okay, so I'm going in. You stay here. I'll be back," before facing the house.

His nerves fired on all cylinders as he walked up the sidewalk, noticing the grass had been freshly cut but that the flowerbeds were bare. The scent of cattle and sunshine hung in the air, and there was no better balm to Carson's soul than that.

After knocking on the door, he only had to wait a few seconds for a redhead to open the door. She was pretty, like the blonde, and yet his heart didn't flounce around in his chest like a fish out of water the way it had at the sight of the other woman.

"Hello," he said, smiling at her. "I'm Carson Chatworth." He extended his hand for her to shake, which she did.

"Come on in," she said, falling back and turning as she walked. "I'm Scarlett Adams. I've got my associates with me today." She pointed to a cowboy sitting at the kitchen table, which had been turned to face the door. "Hudson Flannigan. And Adele Woodruff."

Carson almost fell down at the sight of *Adele Woodruff*—the woman who'd almost hit his truck in the parking lot yesterday. Well, now he knew her name, and he hadn't even had to make any phone calls or toss any money around.

———

Can opposites Carson and Adele make a love connection? Find out in the next book in this series, **Last Chance Cowboy!**

Scan the QR code for a direct link to the paperback.

Liz Isaacson

Last Chance Ranch Romance series

Journey to Last Chance Ranch and meet curvy, mature women looking for love later in life. Experience sisterhood, goat yoga, and a fake marriage against a stunning, inspirational ranch background—and some sexy cowboys too— from USA Today bestseller and Top 10 Kindle All-Star author Liz Isaacson!

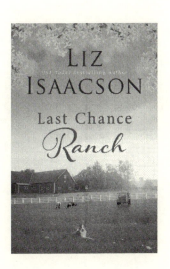

Last Chance Ranch (Book 1): A cowgirl down on her luck hires a man who's good with horses and under the hood of a car. Can Hudson fine tune Scarlett's heart as they work together? Or will things backfire and make everything worse at Last Chance Ranch?

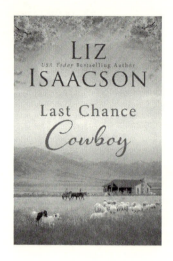

Last Chance Cowboy (Book 2): A billionaire cowboy without a home meets a woman who secretly makes food videos to pay her debts...Can Carson and Adele do more than fight in the kitchens at Last Chance Ranch?

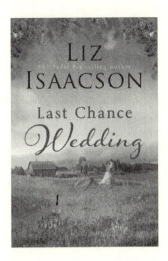

Last Chance Wedding (Book 3): A female carpenter needs a husband just for a few days... Can Jeri and Sawyer navigate the minefield of a pretend marriage before their feelings become real?

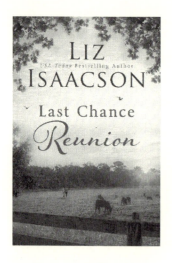

Last Chance Reunion (Book 4): An Army cowboy, the woman he dated years ago, and their last chance at Last Chance Ranch... Can Dave and Sissy put aside hurt feelings and make their second chance romance work?

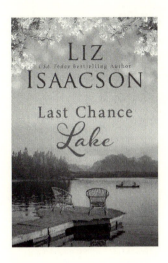

Last Chance Lake (Book 5): A former dairy farmer and the marketing director on the ranch have to work together to make the cow cuddling program a success. But can Karla let Cache into her life? Or will she keep all her secrets from him - and keep *him* a secret too?

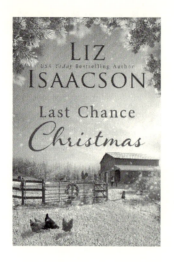

Last Chance Christmas (Book 6): She's tired of having her heart broken by cowboys. He waited too long to ask her out. Can Lance fix things quickly, or will Amber leave Last Chance Ranch before he can tell her how he feels?

About Liz

Liz Isaacson writes inspirational romance, usually set in Texas, or Wyoming, or anywhere else horses and cowboys exist. She lives in Utah, where she writes full-time, takes her two dogs to the park everyday, and eats a lot of veggies while writing. Find her on her website, along with all of her pen names, at feelgoodfictionbooks.com

Made in United States
Troutdale, OR
03/25/2025

30078134R00173